T0064149

Disappearing Fathers

NAUGHTY NICKERS

PARTRIDGE

A Penguin Random House Company

ISBN:	Hardcover	978-1-4828-9569-8
	Softcover	978-1-4828-9567-4
	eBook	978-1-4828-9245-1

To order additional copies of this book, contact
Toll Free 800 101 2657 (Singapore)
Toll Free 1 800 81 7340 (Malaysia)
orders.singapore@partridgepublishing.com

www.partridgepublishing.com/singapore

FOREWORD

I love my Father, I love him the most, and he used to be a bastard too. Well that's only in my opinion and it was just to my mother. I guess really he was just being the Daddy and he was pretty darn good at it too.

Larry, my ol' man, did well for us all, he worked and he worked bloody hard in his day, provided a roof over our heads, food in the cupboards, discipline, car and car maintenance, he did the lot. I s'pose in those days when we were growing up it was just the done thing. **Dad was a jack of all trades** and a **master of most.**

But this story is not about Larry's Life, as wonderful as it was, but about mine, and the wonderful daddys of my children and I s'pose the differences of the times gone by and the expectations we have, the help Single, Homeless, or beaten wives and mothers have these days.

Anyway, **I'm a single mother of 4 to 3 different Bastards.** Actually I was gonna call the book **"The Bastards I have Known"**, but apparently that's been done, so I thought I'd call it **"True Story"**, which it is, each and every word. Finally this title seemed the most appropriate. It's unbelievable at times and when I re-read it, shock myself all over again.

Just to get a piccy on the wonderful life I've had so far, apparently, and only according to nearly every one I know—The best thing that ever happened in my whole life was that the house burnt down.

I had the insurance of course so I got the big twenty thousand dollars. I would have preferred the cash money but the insurance company had a New-For-Old policy. I've still got all those material possessions at this point, but anything's possible round the corner. I guess. **NO NO** it's not. I don't think so. No more for me. **I've had enough, more than enough.** Mostly from boyfriends, males, men, lovers, **HUH! LOVERS!** What a strange word to use for people who do fuck all for you, rob ya blind financially and emotionally, half or most of them would knock you out as quick as look at ya, and even the meekest, mildest, little worm, can and may turn against you in the end. If any of these blokes are one of those wonderful, wonderful, Daddy figures then it can be most painful. The Daddys can hurt because they can steal everything from you in one small swoop. (Or two small swoops as the case may be)

I could only finally start this book—because I know now where it finishes and how. I also know that though good ol' John, Paul, George and Ringo said *"Money Can't Buy Me Love"* it certainly couldn't make anything any worse.

On that note—**HERE'S HOPING.**

CHAPPIE 1

DANNY

We've all gotta start somewhere in our stories so the best place for me to start is from my first true love. I always thought as I was growing up **I'd meet Mr. Right, fall in love, get married and have kids, all in the right order of course. I don't actually think I could have got it any wronger.**

As my father always said, "Do it once, and do it right." Well I must've done it wrong for the last fifteen years, **OK.**

It was all so beautiful in the early days. I was 16 going on 17 and baby **I AM NAI-EVE** willing to care for, willing to share for, what a sick **Puppieee**. The boy's name was Danny, I was his first girl and he was my first boyfriend. He was so good looking young Danny and all the girls in the entire school fancied him. I never noticed 'im at first, well why would I, after all I was 3ft tall and twice as wide and was lucky to spend a weekend down the creek catching guppies with a boy at all. **Any boy.**

Anyway by the time I was 17 I realized that boys did not like you just the way you are and that one must be slim. Right then I thought to myself I'll show these bastards, I'll bloody well change.

A few months and two stone later and I can hear the boys walking behind me. "Look at Nickys' arse, not bad" "She's lookin' good."

Huh! Even in those young days I just thought, well fuck you lot. I wasn't good enough with a big fat arse, so don't come sniffing around now.

But then there was Danny. He was gorgeous. God I loved him. Young love is so unconfused and it was perfection. Uh-Oh! Perfection, I don't think so—surely there's someone to put a spanner in the works and there was his Mother. There was no way in the wildest world that this woman was gonna let me have her son.

On our first ever date we went to the local pictures to see Grease with a couple of other young mates. Before Olivia Newton John even got as far as the first meeting at school with John Travolta, and before the whole cast had gone up, Danny's Mother was dragging the poor Lad out of the cinema by the ear-hole.

It certainly spoilt the first occasion that I saw Grease, but while I was still sniveling in the front row, the gorgeous bloke came back, he'd escaped his Mother's Iron Fist. I almost remember how it felt, like it was yesterday. We got to watch the rest of the show in peace and harmony. Danny's Father picked us up after the show and he dropped me off home as well. (no payment expected)

Danny's Father wasn't the problem though it was Her. She just decided we were too young to be so serious. She did everything to stop us from seeing each other short of pulling Danny out of school. She even tried to run me over one day in her mini, HA HA! As the story evolves you'll realize how bloody silly this would seem.

We stuck together and put up with her shit for about a year I s'pose and then she went away for a weekend down to Sydney. Danny's Father actually liked me and he had no worries about us seeing each other. Danny was allowed to come over to the Island for that particular weekend, he and a few other school chums. It was a great time for us all. We were just young and free. I think there were about 5 other people there as well, but there was really only one person there for me. He felt the same. As the night went on my first love and me found a quiet spot alone. We zipped our sleeping bags together for the first time . . . .

I believe it was about 6.30am and Mommy dearest is kicking me in the guts to try and get her son's sleeping bag out from under me. **HUH! The cheek!** Danny wasn't really a Mummy's Boy though, he was hanging around for awhile to cook brekky for everyone, as planned. Mommy Dearest got a bit game for a moment or so and says to all the other fellow campers. (all of which she knew well) "I spose you lot must've been pretty cold out here last night hey, boys?

I suddenly woke up and found my tongue. **"I wasn't COLD, Mrs. Hard, because I had your lovely son to keep me warm."** Needless to say she was not impressed with that and she packed him up and took him home. I did manage to catch a glimpse of Mr Hard, and the amused smirk on his face.

My darling Danny chucked his wallet out of the Island Taxi so's his chicky babe and the rest could party on. What a Champ! I cried for a long time on this one, Mommy Dearest was not going to let it happen, after a few more school holidays being dragged off to anywhere away from little Nicky, and after a few more bribe sessions and a new surfboard or two, Danny naturally found someone else. Naturally.

Bye-bye love, bye-bye virginity. Bye-bye to everything that was dear to me.

This is growing up. This is growing pains and this was the first real pain I knew. They only got worse.

Go to Chappie two if you can stand it.

CHAPPIE 2

GOON

So now I've apparently grown up—that is to say I'm not a virgin anymore and I have loved and lost, but it's better to have loved and lost than never to have loved at all. **HUH!**

Well I met Master Goon through my sister Malinda and her boyfriend Brett. I think Malinda was upset for me losing my first love and wanted to somehow cheer me up. Initially anyway.

Goon was a very amusing chap to say the least. A laugh a minute in fact, always clowning around. The first night I met him was a big set up I guess, though I didn't realize it at the time. He'd probably been dumped by at least half the planet by the time I met him, but I wasn't to know that was I? He was nothing at all like Danny. He was a bit older, had a car and a license and could pick me up himself, no probs. His mother had no problem at all with who he went out with either. This would definitely make life a lot easier.

I met my sister at her little flat at Rainworth, she was waiting there alone for Brett to come back with Goon and two other people who were coming for the trip up the Coast for the weekend. They both arrived back shortly after I got there. He looked rather thrilled when he first saw me. I thought he wasn't bad either, as first impressions go, all right to look at, at least. Not that looks should mean a bloody thing anyway, but so often it does, as I found out in Chappy one while carrying round that fat arse I used to have. I'm sure and positive if I was a big fat lard right now he would have had a completely different look on his face at first sight.

We were destined for the Coast—The Sunshine Coast, Noosa I think. It was really the first time I'd been out with big sister and out for the whole weekend. This was a real adventure for me. Malinda had left home quite a few months before and I hardly ever saw her anymore. I missed her. I had no one to talk to at home without her there. This weekend was going to be great. I was just so excited about it I couldn't keep still. After the initial meeting we headed off to get the other two people who just happened to be another couple. I kept looking back at Goon, in the rear vision mirror, only while he wasn't looking of course. He was certainly good looking in an unusual sort of way. He was different and far removed from Dickhead, who was Mummy's' Boy now and she could bloody well have him. I did still thought of him a lot though, after all I still saw him every day at school.

I remember that night so clearly even now, and there are many reasons why. We'd been driving for some time and all of a sudden, and for no reason I could fathom, I leaned forward to look at Brett and said, **"Hey Brett you're drink driving"**. Malinda was sitting in the middle and gave me an odd look. Brett had been drinking for the whole of the journey anyway, what was the sudden problem? I had leaned seriously forward and said those exact words, **"Hey Brett you're DRINK DRIVING!"** I don't know why I said it. It just came out of my mouth, just like that. I sat back then and the trip continued. I never thought about that comment again, not till after that weekend.

We arrived at our destination at about 4am because it had taken so long for the whole lot of us to get organized. It was a caravan park somewhere at Noosa Heads, couldn't really see much at this time of the morning though, pitch black it was, no moon at all. All 6 of us had a few drinks by then, even little me. I also think I had my first toke on a joint, I'm not sure on that one though because I was pretty pissy on one or two drinks in those days. We were so young and naive, my silly sister and me, we really had no idea about life or about boys at all.

I can't quite remember how it all came about but, Master Goon and I ended up in a sort of closed off caravan room chatting. I like to chat. It was his way I think he made me feel at ease or maybe it was just the few beers I'd had earlier. Goon was a very amusing character as I've said. We told sick jokes and laughed a lot, we were just getting to know each other for a while. Then of course the crunch must come. **The bit where male wants female.** I could not possibly be up for this sort of caper, because deep down I still (silly billy) loved Danny. So being the sort of person I am, I explained to Goon about Chappy 1 and how recent it was. Fortunately for me he was an understanding chap and did not push the issue. We continued to chat on for what was left of the night, and we laughed and laughed a hell of a lot. I really enjoyed his company. He was a pommy you know! They're always funny, I should know.

Next two days was a whirr of pubs and beaches and people, and more pubs, beaches and people. I know I got serious sunburn anyway, I think we all did. Finally the weekend came to an end and I was dropped off at my house. I was sort of relieved in a way, because it was all new to me and really I was quite **shy . . . , THEN!**

"Bye, see ya later. Thanks a lot for the lovely weekend." A quick exchange of phone numbers, and they were gone. Mum and Dad were obviously on the Island for the weekend so I was home alone. Boo hoo! Maybe I started to hate being alone from that moment on.

There was a note on the door from my best friend, **PLEASE RING ME. RAILEEN.** I got in doors and was overcome by this powerful urge to ring my true love, Danny. His words were to be the biggest shock of my life so far.

"Have you heard the news? Glen and Brett are dead." were his exact words.

Shock! I dropped the phone. Some time went by. I picked the phone up and put it back on the receiver, I remember doing that much. I got a tea towel, I think, and then I didn't cry, which I thought I would. I just sat there feeling sort of numb.

Glen and Brett were in Grade 10 the same as the rest of us, our whole lives ahead to do with whatever we chose. They had been two of the fellows who spent the weekend on the Island not so very long ago. Glen was the Fonze of our school, if you know what I mean. Actually I had been secretly in love with him since the beginning of high school, up until I went out with Danny anyway. Oh my God. They can't be gone. They just can't be. Not Glen, No not Glen. This can't be right. I was still sitting on the seat by the phone, staring into space when there was a knock on the door. Danny, my gorgeous Danny. The one I'd loved so much. Those big beautiful eyes of his, now full of pain and torment. His two closest friends in the entire world had been taken from him and from all of us. Here was my Danny, who'd escaped from his mother's clutches once more and was here to comfort his little Darling in a time of grief. What a wonderful young bloke he was. We fell into each other's arms and consoled each other. We hugged each other so tightly that night and we cried together for our friends—lost so young and so ready for life ahead. Once again there was a rude awakening, Mrs. Hard was interrupting this time, by telephone. "Hello, I know he's there, just tell him to get straight home." She hung up.

The end factor was that he did run straight home to Mummy—she had won. I had already finished this one anyway. God how did I get back to this?

After he was gone, I was so messed up. So sad, so lost. I did not want to be alone. I rang Goon. He came immediately to my *emotional rescue,* and I cried and cried on his manly shoulders. He cheered me up a bit, in his funny way and he even had me laughing a bit. He really got me through a very bad time in my life. He spent the rest of the night holding me and finally I slept.

I didn't see him for a while after that night, or it could have been day, I really wouldn't have the foggiest idea. I just know I didn't see him for quite some time. There was a lot going on though, it was just a depressing time for me and a sad ending to the final year of high school for the lot of us. I won't go on about this morbid bit and I'm sure no one wants to read such sad stuff anyway. I will tell you of my only eerie experience in life though, because this is when it happened. You see it concerned Glen.

I was awakened from sleep a couple of days after the funeral—just sat straight up in bed. I sat there for a while and adjusted my eyes. I don't know what woke me. I looked around the room and nothing seemed to be out of order, seemed no reason I had woken. Then I thought I heard something outside the window, so I walked over and looked all round outside—nothing. Then I hear something outside again, I couldn't say what. A hic-up, a whisper, a rustle of the trees, who knows. I also thought I could see something and I don't know what that was either **but something, definitely something.** Then a sudden feeling of stupidity, and again sadness, and grief. I went to walk away from the window, and there on the window ledge was a ring. The ring Glen had given to me on the Island about a year before. I couldn't believe my eyes. **UNBELIEVEABLE** I had thrown that ring. I was so upset with Glen one day, because I'd always fancied him and he always fancied some other . . . He did like me though, but just good friends. I know for sure—True Story—I threw that ring as far as I could throw it. It would have been at least two houses away probably, but there it was, on that window ledge. This is my only ghost story and a true story it is too, as is the rest of this bloody book.

A few weeks after this Danny came round to see me and so did Goon. Firstly Danny came round on his skate-board and he was out the front of the house skateboarding around and then Goon pulls up in his Ford Falcon. Well what is a girl to do. It was fairly obvious to me. I told both of them, I could not possibly choose between them and they could both leave. They both did, but Goon came back for more and as I had already said earlier—Danny was over.

Goon and I had lots of good times—*we went everywhere man, we went everywhere.* We used to go out to Lakeside a lot. He liked to get stoned and watch or sleep through the races, whether it was cars or bikes didn't matter to him. Actually he used to get stoned and laugh at me a lot. I never quite understood this one, but he usually made me laugh in the end. Obviously after awhile every male is gonna want **MORE.** What is more? you may ask yourself, well, we all want more but for men more means **SEX.** Well I never. How fucking unusual, for a bloke to want more. Oh sorry, my thoughts on men have jumped about 10 years. I spose it's OK for a young lad of 23 to want this of his 18 year old girlfriend, especially if they actually like each other as well.

I can't remember all that well about this particular incident, but I know when I finally did succumb to his wants and needs I thought it was allright. I'm with him now, we're together, we've been together for quite some time, and we'll be together forever. We did the deed. It wasn't too bad, though I can't see why we should do it in his car in the Cemetery at Rosalie, perhaps he's religious, oh who cares—the guy loves me. As it turned out he loved one or two others before me. Happy Birthday Nicky, *you can cry if you want to, cry if you want to, cry if you want to.* I bloody well did too because Goon had given me crabs for my 18th birthday. That's all I got too, nothing else, no card, no pressy, no nothing, just crabs. **YUK YUK YUK . . .**

I was very naive and actually as I've got older, I would not call it naive at all. I'd call it blatantly stupid! Goon rang again and I of course went off my brain and said I did not want to see him anymore. He explained that he must have had them before me and just didn't realize it. He was terribly sorry and would make it up to me. **"Please give me another chance."** I did.

He arrived at my place to pick me up sort of late on the Friday night. He drove up the driveway and beeped the horn. Dad would not under any circumstances let me go down to him. (He obviously knew nothing of the crabs)

"You're not going with that bloke until he comes up the stairs and escorts you out. No Way!" Well I slithered past Dad somehow and was down the stairs in seconds. Much to my horror here was Goon with his mate, and his mate was obviously staying in the front seat. HUH! Well! I'd just been made a complete arse of, and in front of Dad if I walk back up the stairs, so I have to jump in the back, don't I. Off we go into the City somewhere—I suggest a place, his mate says no good, Goon suggested another place but that was no good either and on it goes all the way to town. By the time we got to town I'd had more than enough, if I'm not going to let Dad tell me what to do and where to go then I'm certainly not going to listen to this pair of idiots. I got out of the car at some set of lights and went partying on my own. I think maybe that night set the rest of my life for me. **I still think that it's easier to party on your own, with no one to tell you it's time to come home or who with or why.**

No crabs today my love has gone away, his company was gay, until I went away.

CHAPPIE 3

BUSHLANDER MICK

School was well over by this time and I had been working in a Delicatessen for about 10 months. I remember when I got this job because my mum was yelling and screaming at me about getting a job, and I was lying on my bed reading a book. She yelled out, "You won't get a job lying on your bed you know."

About 5 minutes later, if that, the phone rang and it was Mrs. Rob to offer me a part-time job at Stafford Deli. I accepted and said I'd be there tomorrow.

"Well, there ya go Mother Duck I can get a job while lying on my bed." After all I'd put in heaps and heaps of effort to get a job and I'd been for nearly every job going, in the whole area.

After the 10 months or so the old couple sold that shop and the new owners had their own staff, so that was the end of that. Then I got a wonderful job in Coles, like half the rest of the population of this planet. I got sacked from there for apparently stealing a dollar, which of course I did not. I guess they were just over staffed, but **it's hardly likely a person would steal ONE lousy dollar** and risk a huge **$82.50** a week. I was pretty happy about this anyway and I kept all my holiday pay to take myself off to Lorraine Martin Business College.

Well I did my 10week course and we were promised (then in the 80's just like now in the 90's) a job, after receiving a Diploma for secretarial work. There was no help after the course, of course, because they now have your money, or mine in their pocket, why would they help any more. I trudged around the city for weeks knocking on doors and showing resumes, wearing stockings and high heels, make-up and hair in a near bun, you name it I tried it, but at that time failed to find a receptionist/ typist type job.

I got sick and tired of walking the city streets so went for the next job going, Harding Brothers. This was not at all what I wanted but we all have to make money and survive. It was conveyor belts, going flat out. Packing sugar of every description. Dried fruits and chickpeas and it was all **bloody hard work done at flat out speeds.** The place was full of women of every shape and size. I met a good friend while I was there named Danielle, she was a bit younger than I was, but we got on really well. We chatted away while we worked. We used to sing silly songs and play games and stuff to pass the time in this very dull job. We chatted about all sorts, like ya do in a factory and she told me how she had just been dragged from everything she ever new in New Zealand and brought to this horrible huge hot country. All because her mother wanted to come over here and said there were better opportunities here for Danielle and Mick her brother.

Danielle and I chatted about Mick then and she reckoned that he and I would be perfect for each other, although Mick was apparently still possibly in love with a young lass he'd left behind. After a few weeks of her trying to convince me I finally gave in and Mick had also agreed to meet me. It was gonna be a blind date, my first blind date. How exciting! We had arranged it for the following Friday Night.

We met in Brisbane City outside a Fun Parlor because this was the only place that Danielle or Mick knew how to find. I remember the look on his face as I came up the street and was close enough to see what I was looking at and Danielle was nodding furiously in his direction. The closer I got the broader his smile. It was one of those love at first sight scenarios, for us both.

Mick was very good looking, probably enough to be a male model, as far as I was concerned anyway. He was tall and had the beautiful tanned skin that Maoris do, along with those lovely brown eyes. He was half pakeha and half Maori, which some how made him even better looking than most Maoris. Only in my opinion of course.

We went to a few different discos as they were all called then whether it was disco music or not. I had an absolutely wonderful night and I was completely besotted by Michael Tunifwha and wanted to see him as often as possible. The night ended too soon for my liking and I had to wait all week to see Mick again. It was the longest week of my life. Finally the weekend would come around and I'd get to see my darling Mick again.

After awhile the weekends started on Thursdays, before we even noticed it happening. The three of us went to Brothers Leagues Club on a regular basis after awhile, every Thursday Night. This is a point, which changed my life. Mick got a bit too drunkish one night, meaning he was over the limit. He'd just bought an XT 250 brand spanking new and had to take me home about five K's and then take himself and his sister back the 30 odd K's to West End. After some discussion I convinced the pair of them they could lob on Mum's lounge floor or something and leave early in the morning. Anything is better than being done by the cops or worst still ending up dead. Danielle and I were still working together and we could leave together for work and Mick could find his own way home then.

Well there was no problems with any of this till about 3am when my dear ol' Dad woke up and came out and said, "Who's that here, Nicky?. You've woken me up, so the lot of you can sod off and you can go with them in the morning."

We had been sitting there as quiet as mice and I'm positive he'd just woken up by himself. Danielle was already asleep on a mattress on the floor and Mick and I were sitting fully dressed on the lounge watching a late movie. So morning comes and my Mother gets up and offers scrambled eggs and bacon to Danielle, Mick and me before our hard day's work. Everything seemed to be cool at the breakfast table. We organized for my brother to drive me and Danielle to work and Mick just had to get himself home then. I thought everything had blown over with Dad. Apparently not—as I was leaving he says,

"I want you and all your shit out of here by the time we get back from Macleay Island on Sunday night". BOOM BOOM!

So I go do my eight hour day at Harding Brothers and I'm spinning out all day about what to do. What do I do next? My darling Father has thrown me out, shit, *and I'm only 19.* Danielle wanted me to move in with them and reckoned it would be all right with her Mum. In fact, she said it would make things a bit better financially. I went home with Danielle to work out the next part of my life. Between the pair of them (Danielle and Mick) they convinced me I was best off to move in with them and their Mum and the little sister, Trudy who was about 7 or 8. Well I was in love for a start, which made the decision much easier for me. On Friday afternoon— that same afternoon, I was leaving home. **Leaving my Mummy and Daddy and going out into the big wide world.** The 2 people who had raised me, fed me and clothed me had now requested that I leave. I was a blithering mess but I had my true love and my friend to help me through. Mick borrowed his Mum's car for the big move. I took **"all my shit"** and I left. I also left a photo on the bed in a folder which had the word *"MEMORIES"* written on the front. I thought my Mum would fancy that when she got home from the Island.

I didn't contact my parents for a couple of weeks after that. I just cruised along through work and saving and friends and my new life with Danny, Mick, Trudy and their Mum. It was a completely new world for me. An eye opener I s'pose you could say. Mum went to work at some ungodly hour like we all did, somewhere round daylight. Trudy went to a lady down the road for a few hours before school so she had to get up early too the poor girl. Actually when Danny and I walked down Brunswick Street, The Valley, to the train, many mornings it was still pitch black. Thank Christ I was too young and stupid to be scared about this state of affairs, at the time. I guess Mick and the family were none the wiser about the Valley either because they were fresh from New Zealand.

We continued on like this for a couple of months and then Mick lost his job. He went here and there and everywhere looking for work but no luck. One day when Danielle and I got home from work he told us he'd decided to go to Mt Isa and get a job in the mines. He had an Uncle and some other relatives up there and they said there was heaps of work, but only for men. And with that off he went and I decided to go home to Mummy's again because I no longer felt welcome in his family's home without him there.

My Mother was more than pleased to have me home again, and even said so, but I was not happy anymore I just wanted Mick to come back. I missed him so much even though he wrote a lot and rang a lot as well. I just couldn't get him out of my mind. He begged me to jump on a train every time he was on the phone. **"I love you so much Nicky, I'll look after you."** Eventually he got the better of me and I quit my very dull and boring job on the chain gang and organized a train to Mt Isa as soon as possible. I didn't tell him any of this though—or anyone else for that matter, only my parents. I wanted it to be the surprise of his life!

I was so jumpy for the long two-day journey north into insecurity and No Mans' Land. Christ it seemed like the never-ending journey. It was a rude awakening when it did finally come to an end. It was blistering heat of 40 degrees or more in the shade and there wasn't a living soul anywhere to point me in any direction—let alone the right one. Finally a taxi appeared out of nowhere and I dived into it with all my worldly possessions and gave the bloke the address. I was so excited, I could hardly breathe as we pulled into the Caravan Park that Mick had been staying at with his Uncle.

So here I am 2000miles later, Little Nicky, 19 years old standing outside my lover's caravan with all my shit and guess what, the surprise is on me, Mick, is not home. His Uncle came out with the Mrs. His Uncle just took one look at me and went **OH SHIT!** And put his hand over his mouth in horror, like I obviously shouldn't be there. Where is he, where's Mick, I managed to say, tears welling up in my eyes. His Uncle said, **"He's moved out and got a place with some Lady down the road."**

"Where have you just come from?"

"Brisbane." is all I could blurt out at this stage.

Mick's Uncle stepped up to-me then and put his arm around me and without laughing too hard said, **"I was only joking, Nicky, He's just down the Pub drowning his sorrows because he misses you so much."**

Pete, and I think her name was Anna, both hugged me and made me more than welcome. We put my stuff in their van and then headed off to town to find Mick.

When we got to the third daggy looking pub, Pete spotted Mick and told me to hide behind the duke box, for a second till he said hello. Mick had his back to the doorway and was just sitting hunched over at the bar. I did hide behind the duke box after putting on *Dream, Dream, Dream, When I want you in the night, when I want you to hold me tight, Whenever I want you all I have to do is Dree-e-e-eam.* Mick turned sadly round as **"Our Song"** came on. When Pete got over to him I jumped up in the background and his face lightened up like nothing I've ever seen before, seconds and we were in each other's arms once more. It was a gorgeous moment, it was euphoric. It was the greatest feeling I've ever felt. **It was forever. It was perfect—Uh, Oh, here we go again. Can I be wrong again? No, not this time, this is the one, it's too wonderful to ever change.**

I was deliriously happy and I had found the man to spend the rest of my life with. Life went on in this wonderful loving blissfully happy state for a couple of months. The only problem we had at all was money. Mick had not found work up here as he had hoped, so we were both broke. I wasn't too bothered about the no job bit because I'd only thrown in a shit Kickers job anyway to be with the one I loved.

We moved out of Pete and Ann's' van and into a Donger, which is a very small tin shed about 10 by 10. It was a bit daggy, but it was ours alone. We had a lovely time together even though we had no funds. We used to sneak into the showers late at night so we could shower together. We lazed around the pool most of the day after checking the papers for jobs, usually with no success. After only a few short weeks Mick decided that if there was no work up here we may as well travel back again, to Brisbane. I didn't mind either way as long as we were together. He wanted to travel the distance on his XT 250 as well, which would definitely be an adventure. Oh my God, 2000 miles or more on an XT 250, it's an impossibility, or is it? We were doing it anyway, much to my horror.

"Mick Darling, we could put the bike and us on the train and be home in a couple of days". He wasn't having it though. He wanted to explore the wide-open spaces of Australia. I could hardly blame him, I was just thinking of my poor arse at the time.

So at about 11pm on some evening in 1981, Bushlander Mick and I set off on the trek from Mt Isa to Brisbane. I left with a pillow under my arse, but that didn't last long. It caught on fire by the time we got to "Mary Kathleen", which is only about 10 to 15 minutes up the road. I had to give that idea a miss from then on. Our belongings were made up of 1 two man tent, 1 boogie box, 1 gun (don't know what sort) a bag of clothes each, 2 yellow heavy duty rain coats, a couple of woolen blankets *and a partridge in a pear tree.* **Ha! Ha!**

On and on and on we went through all sorts of tiny little out-back towns that no one has ever heard of before, least of all me. The roads had nothing at all to look at either, not a single thing, not even a tree for miles and miles. There wasn't even a cow or two, only dead ones which started to worry me a bit.

If we broke down out here we could be here to stay. We finally got to Townsville and I was pleased to be off those out-back roads, it was quite scary really. Mick didn't seem to notice though, he was on a mission, and that was that. I s'pose he had it in his head to tell all the Maori mates of his big adventure in Oz. It's hard to remember all the dreary details, but I think we stayed in a caravan park there, but only in our two-man tent. I was still blissfully happy, though I was cold, wet, hungry and had a fucking sore arse. I could hardly get off the motorbike. It really wasn't the sort of motor bike you do 200 miles on let alone 2000.

We left Townsville at some early hour once again. It's always best to leave before dawn because it's the coolest time of day. Man. Not this time though. It was cool allright, but it was also pissing down. Great. I thought Mr. Bushlander would stop after awhile, but on and on and on he went again, in the blinding rain this time, with me hugging in closely behind. Hour after hour he rode on until we got to the next big town—Mackay. Yahoo! We'll stop here for a while I thought.—No—Wrong. We'll fuel, a quick leg stretch and on we go. We were getting seriously low on money by now and would have to stop somewhere eventually to get a dole cheque or some help from the Saint Vinnies or someone.

When we got to Sarina, we stopped at a Second Hand shop to sell the boogie box and the gun so we could continue on. The people at the shop offered $10 each. No way this was enough, the cassette player was brand new and the gun was definitely worth at least $50, so we turned down the money and continued on towards Rocky.

About half way to Rockhampton the roads were blocked off due to floodwaters. Well this stopped Mr. Fucking Bushlander Mick in his tracks. So back we go. I had seriously had enough by this time, as you can imagine, and furthermore I could no longer feel my arse at all.

Other than that, the fish that we'd caught yesterday at breakfast time had disagreed with me. The fish was Catfish. Maybe that had something to do with it. The Catfish in New Zealand was probably OK, but this was not. My face was puffed up like a beach ball and I could hardly see either, and I felt a bit weird as well. We went back to the second hand shop to try and get the pittance for our gear, there was no choice now.

Knock, knock on the door of the house now, because the shop had been shut for an hour or so and now we'd have to go interrupt them at their house.

"We'll have the money you offered earlier for the gun and the cassette player please," I said.

The bloke at the door stood there for a moment, and then said, "Oh shut up and come inside, you poor buggers."

This lovely old couple, Ethel and Gordon, felt sorry for us and let us in to their home. I was so wrapped.

First it was, "In the shower with you both, and then Ethel will have a nice bowl of soup for you." In the shower we went. It was the best shower that I reckon I ever had. They had no problems about us showering together either. Well after all we were travelling across the country together anyway. When we got out, Ethel did have soup for us, pea and ham, my favorite. Then there were the huge slabs of fresh home baked bread as well. Yum. Yum. I was absolutely starving. This was Heaven on Earth. It definitely was heaven after a thousand or so miles on the back end of a motor bike.

Mick and I stayed for nearly a week in the end. We got on really well with Ethel and Gordon and also we still had no choice, because we had to wait for the floodwaters to subside and also we were now waiting on a cheque from the government. We did all sorts of things while we were there. Went out to see the cane being burnt off, went to the beach, met heaps of friends of Gordon's and enjoyed our time off the road. Ethel and Gordon would not even take the cassette player or the gun when we left, they said it was so nice to meet such a nice young couple, and wished us all the best for the future.

Get back on that bike and ride, Nicky—and off we go again. I vaguely remember staying in Rocky under someone's house the next night. We had to stay there too for an extra day because the shitty, poxy, little trail bike had done a sprocket and the poxy, shitty bike shop had to send to Brisbane for it. Fish for tea again. Here goes my luck again. I got poisoned. My face puffed up again, like a puffer fish or a toadfish or something and I was so crook. Ahhh! Urrrrrr! It was really bad, but I survived, and on we went.

The rest of the trip is mostly a blur but I do know for sure that the true love had dwindled quite a bit by the time we got home. Home, being my Mother's house, which is the only real home I know.

This time we both stayed there. Mum made my bed up and made another one on the floor for Mick. We changed it to a double on the floor each night and Mum changed it every day. Mum was really glad to have me home again and made allowances for this in the end. She realized we'd been sleeping together for months now anyway what was the point of worrying.

Dad gave Mick a job painting the house, which gave him a bit of money to play with and it also paid for his keep. There ended up being a drama here though because Dad reckoned that Mick was trying to rip him off, because he wasn't getting it done fast enough. It was sort of my fault because I'd tell him to come in and have a rest, for awhile and watch the mid-day movie with me. I tried to tell Dad this but he wouldn't listen. Out went Mick. This time I stayed home.

The whole relationship became very casual and I was a bit put out by his nonchalant attitude. I still loved him—I guess I expected too much.

I thought he'd get us a place, not go back to his mother and sisters again. Next thing he got a flat with his mate and I was even more hurt than before. Soon after this it was Mick's 20th Birthday, so I thought I'd go all out for this occasion and organized a surprise party for him with the help of his flat mate Lee. It was a nice collection of friends, some of his, some of mine, and a few work mates. I arrived a bit before Mick finished work, with my best mate from college. Mick had just started a new job with an insurance company so he was on top of the world. I bought him a new silk suit as well so he would look just the part on Monday, when he turned up.

Then he arrived home. He seemed to be pretty happy when he saw all his mates there to wish him a Happy Day, and he was well impressed with the silk suit. Everything was going great. I prepared most of the food earlier with the help of Lee (The Chef) and there was nothing left to do but enjoy. I was just playing hostess with the mostess, and making sure that everyone was having a good time etc. I realized we'd run out of wine for the punch, not to worry—there's a pub less than a block away. So off I go to get some more, needless to say I was getting a bit pissy by this stage.

There were still a few cars parked around the front of the flats I noticed as I walked down the driveway. Karen's car was still there too. Mmm, I thought she'd gone. I went over towards it and then it seemed like I was in a trance from that moment on. There they were—my beautiful darling Mick and my Best Mate—doing it, making love, **bonking, fucking, screwing, rooting** whatever you'd like to call it. Oh my God! Oh my God! No. No this can't be possible. Not my Mick. The pain went through me and my whole chest felt like it was gonna explode or cave in. I couldn't breathe, speak or scream. This is not happening to me, not to me. Not my gorgeous bike riding Mick, my future Husband and the father of my children. Nooooooow!

I backed slowly away from the car and was not seen by either of the happy couple. My feet moved, one foot in front of the other. They took me up the stairs. I walked through the flat and through to the kitchen. I grabbed the largest knife off the collection on the wall. (Mr. Chef had them displayed) I went slowly back down the stairs and round the back of the flats this time. I found myself in an empty old tin shed.

I must've had some light in there because I remember staring at my hand, my left hand. I stared for a long time. I ran the knife slowly and lightly across my little finger, kind of like I was playing. Then I stared at the beads of dark red blood I thought it would be blue, build up and drip onto the dirt floor. My head was saying I don't wanna be here, I just can't be here, I don't wanna be here, I just don't, repeated over and over, again and again. And then from nowhere down came this crashing knife, ker-thwack! Down it went and into my wrist. The blood started to pump. It was quite amazing to watch. 1, 2, 3, squirt, squirt, squirt. I watched it for awhile. Then I seemed to wake up as I watched it pumping out across the dimly lit shed. The pain in my hand seemed to overpower the rest of the pain in my heart and I suddenly realized that life itself was pumping out of me. I dropped the knife and went back towards the stairs to the flat once more.

I apparently got to the second flight of stairs and passed out.

My next memory was at the Royal Brisbane Hospital in the waiting area, waiting for stitches. Danielle was with me. She was pushing me in a wheelchair. Danny was trying to make light of the situation and she was also pretty pissed herself. She pushed me up and down the corridors and was being silly and laughing her head off, and doing the occasional 360o in the hall, until my name was called. I watched intently, as they sewed up what would have been the biggest mistake of my life. Fortunately for me they thought I'd fallen down the stairs with a bottle or something, otherwise they would have locked me up in the Nutcase Ward, and thrown away the key. Who could really blame them.

Mick and his flat mate turned up at some point while I was in with the Doctors. Then my wonderful, wonderful Mick offered me a sausage roll. Great! Well that should bloody well fix everything up. All I could find the strength to say was, Go, just please go. They all went then and I was alone. I left the Hospital and headed for home. My Mum's home. I walked then. All I wanted to do was to go Home. I walked and I thought. I did a hell of a lot of thinking. Never again will I get so hung up. Never again will I fall in love. I walked the 10 to 15 miles walk from the hospital to my Mum's No one was there as usual. I guess I was relieved anyway. I broke into the house and crawled into bed and CRIED.

It's over.

CHAPPIE 4

NED KELLY
(A SHORT INTERLUDE)

A couple of years went by till I was even remotely interested in anyone. I guess the way this sounds is that I'm a co-dependant person. Well p'raps I am. I've never actually thought about it till just recently and it was pointed out by my best friend of today, when I told her about this book. It's probably because each episode I speak of in my life is a time with a male or partner.

I honestly feel that I've always been better off alone. Maybe I'm happier when someone's telling me how wonderful I am, but it's all bullshit in the end isn't it, and besides all that, they (they being men) never tell you anything nice these days anyway, so what's the f—ing point. Germain Greer has a lot to answer for I reckon—I'd be happier if she had left well enough alone, and men were still men and women were running the show like they have for centuries.

Anyhow back to the drab story. I believe I met Mr. Ned Kelly at the Jazz 'n Jug session at the Caxton Hotel. I was having a ball anyway. The Jazz and Jug says it all really. I wasn't really interested in men anymore so I just enjoyed myself. God it was a great Pub in those days.

Everyone used to sit on the side of the hill and watch the band. I used to dance with this bloke every week when we were there. He was a great dancer in this style, he could throw me all over the place and somehow make it look good. He never lost grip either, and I never once got thrown off into the crowd. Then along came Ned. I don't remember the exact moment I met him. Silly isn't it. (I've remembered him ever since) He was exactly my height. He was sort of silly looking in a way, with big bulging eyes, blonde hair, what was left of it, and a reddish sort of moustache.

A happy man. I s'pose, thinking of it now, he was very boyish and he made me feel like I should look after him—or at the very least, give him a big hug. Which I did. He and I both had tickets to see the Clash that night at Cloudland, so we decided to go on from the Caxton together.

After catching a cab from pub A to Cloudlands (which is no longer there) Ned rolled a very large joint before we went in. I had some with him. He seemed so casual really the way he just sat on a log and rolled up, and then passed it on to me. It would have seemed wrong to knock it back. Everyone else always tried to shove it down your throat. After this large joint, we went in and just mingled in through the crowd like it was a game. He was ahead and using a sort of creeping through the jungle motion, and turning round every so often to shush, me and then to gesture me onwards, like all was OK up ahead. We got up to the front of the crowds like this and I s'pose if I was thinking of it at the time, he was in the army and on a mission to get to the front.

He was another who made me laugh, and if I wasn't laughing out loud I was at least smiling. After the Clash and Cloudland, the excitement wasn't over and he took me on to a place called Pipps.

"I'll have a beer, thank you" I said.

"No way, Nicky, you order something completely different," he replied.

"But I never drink anything but beer," I told him again.

So he ordered a **"Green Monster"**, which he made up on the spot, Galliano, Green Vok, Vodka and a splash of orange juice.

Yummo! I used to drink that drink quite a lot at $5 a pop, but that was only with this lovely little man. I stayed at a flat he was staying at with a few others. After a few coffees and a smoke on the front verandah in the morning, overlooking the Valley, I left and went home. Oh dear here we go again. I couldn't stop thinking about him all week long. I absolutely had to rush over there on Saturday morning to see what they were doing, well Ned mainly. Judy answered the door with her mate, Jo behind her.

"Come in Nick, how ya going".

"Well I mainly came over to see Ned, is he about?"

They looked at each other momentarily and then Judy said,

"He's gone home to the trouble and strife, wife"

What a dopey cow I was. Those pair looked at each other like it was as plain as the nose on your face. They told me he wasn't exactly married but he did have a woman and a kid as well, and he'd gone home.

Another one's gone another one's gone and another one bites the dust. That song came out around this time and seemed to fit the time in my life.

CHAPPIE 5

WONDERFUL DADDY THE 1ST

After meeting Judy and Jo, I got to know a few more people around the flats, and Tracey, my best mate from High School, and I hung around these parts quite a bit. The Spring Hill area in those days seemed to be full of Army fellas or Uni Students. I was quite smitten with a cockney Pomme next, but he had to go back to London soon so there wasn't much point pursuing that one.

I turned 20 at this point and Mum and Dad were selling our family home to move full-time to Macleay Island. They decided to throw my big 21st type party then because it would be too awkward the following year to do it from the Island. No worries at all, I thought. So I planned my party and invited all the people from the flats and all me old mates. Tracey had by this time hooked up with Trevor, another A. J. (Army Jerk) and he brought his flat mate with him. He's not bad, I thought to myself, but he'd brought someone with him. Bummer! We danced and we drank, and played a few silly games, and danced and drank some more. Towards the end of the night a few of us, me being the main offender, decided to go into town, Night Clubbing. Potter, Trevor's flat mate, ditched the chic he brought with him, (he sent her home in a cab) and came into town with the rest of us. Me mainly, God I was gorgeous then, I just wished I realized it.

Potter and I went out together for a few weeks. He was a Uni Student studying Computer Engineering and he also had a good job at Sperry Univac, which later became Unysis. I was working in the Tax Department by this stage so at least I had a half-decent job. Potter was a good-looking chap with seriously curly hair, which he hated and a thick moustache. He was of slight build with a bit of a potbelly or beer gut, not too much though and he was a bit taller than me and a year older. Everything seemed to fit in pretty perfectly.

We went out a lot in those early days. One night after coming home from a good night out with the ol' mates, we were laughing and joking in bed and Potter said,

"Will you marry me?"

Just like that. Out of the blue it was.

Answer.

"Yes, Yes I will."

Then he dashed off to get a bottle of 12-year-old port that he got for his 21ˢᵗ. We were both blissfully happy and then all of a sudden he was all upset and told me he used to have a brother and wished he was here to share the moment of joy with him. We both cried for his little brother who died at the age of 3. Who was to know, that was the closest sweetest moment that Potter and I ever shared. And who was to know the significance of this little boy who had passed on, his name was Stuart.

The next step of course is the most terrifying in a young girl's life and that is meeting the future in-laws. The Mother-in-law. I feel it's much worse for a girl—because they (Mother and son) expect so much of this poor young lass. Especially when they're so bloody good at everything, and I mean everything. His Mother was a marvelous cook, she kept an immaculate house, was a nurse and matron, a seamstress and dressmaker, a cake decorator and she did all this with 6 children. Meemar was the perfect Mother and Wife. I had to meet up to all this at the ripe old age of 21.

After a few months we moved in together with his mate, Trevor, and Trevor's fiancée (who was not my best friend from school). We announced our engagement with a huge party and life was absolutely wonderful. The 4 of us got on pretty well, but this did not last long. The other chicky babe started to piss me right off. She was so tight and so stuck up, it was also fairly obvious she looked down her long thin nose at me. So after a short time Potter and I got a flat. Our own little flat with our own stuff.

We both worked all week and lazed around on weekends at the flat mostly and did the usual boring chores that build up when you're out all week. I started to realize that I was actually doing all the chores and that he was doing all the lazing around in front of the box. To me life seemed to be getting in a sort of a rut and so soon. I wanted to have parties and go out dancing and stuff like we used to not so long ago. When we did do anything, it always seemed to be evenings at HIS Sisters' and HIS Mother's or at home in BED.

I know, I know, I should have been deliriously happy and over the moon in love, but I was not. I started to wonder if I was in love with the idea of marriage and kids and not so much in love with the bloke who'd actually asked me to marry him. Then it happened! **He hit me. A few times.** He also threw me in the shower to cool me off. It's a fucking pity he'd put the hot water on and not the cold and so scalded me, causing me to kick the shower siding out which was unfortunately made of glass. It shattered and went everywhere and I was obviously now in quite a bit of pain. Don't get me wrong about all this. I wasn't an innocent bystander here, because I was half way drunk and wanted to go out partying somewhere. Possibly I deserved it, maybe I didn't. Who really cared, I still went out anyway. What's new. It's my life isn't it and when your beliefs are—"You only live once", Then why should anyone ever try to slow you down or stop you from doing what you want. I guess I figured Mr. Right wouldn't, so therefore this must be Mr. Wrong, or at least NOT Mr. Right. I think a slap in the face does wonders to wake one up to one's silly self.

I did stay with Potter for awhile after this incidence, it wouldn't seem right otherwise. My father had laid out quite a bit of money for the intended Wedding Reception and the cars. The cars were to be a Mercedes for the riff-raff and a Roller for Larry and me to arrive in. The only condition (and there always was one) was a few photos of Dad behind the wheel, for him to send his big Brother. I can relate to that, the bleedin' show-off.

Another incident happened as the wedding got closer. We were s'posed to go and see the Preacher on a particular evening after a long day at work. I put a tin of Spaghetti Bolognaise on to heat up and then just boiled some ordinary spaghetti to go with it and I also had some garlic bread. Not too bad a meal for a quick number before going out. Not good enough though, not for Mr. Flaming Perfect. He said, **"You're not giving me some shit out of a can I hope."**

To which I replied, **"Fuck you Potter, you can do what you like about dinner."**

Then I stomped into the bedroom and locked the door. I also left the dinner boiling on the stove, and had no concern whatever about the pots boiling dry and turning black.

"Nicky, come on, we've got to see the Preacher in about half an hour."

"Fuck the Preacher too and the Fucking wedding.

I heard Potter ring the Preacher and explain we couldn't make it tonight and made some excuse for why. A couple of hours went by. Knock, knock on the door again.

"Come on Nick, I'm sorry, please open the door I want to go to bed."

I opened the door. After a while he told me he was hungry. HUH! So I got up and this time I got out a packet of 2-minute noodles. You should have seen the look on his face. I just said, "Don't say one word Potter or you'll end up with them on your head."

He ate the noodles and thanked me very much.

The next week my mother, my Best Friend and I were all in the City to pick out and purchase wedding shoes and shoes for the bridesmaids. I had already picked up a Wedding Dress at the local markets for $25. I was stuffing around a lot and mum finally had to go home, and home she went. At this point I said to Tracey, **"Fuck the wedding shoes and fuck the wedding, there isn't going to be one"**

To which Tracey replied, "I've been waiting months to hear you say that."

We hugged each other and cried a bit and then spent the night on the piss together. A couple of days later while Potter was at work, I packed all my worldly possessions and moved into a flat with a work friend Donna and her boyfriend, whose name escapes me. This was a really hard time for me. I really missed Potter so much. I guess you just get used to the one person around all the time even if it isn't love. Potter rang often, and I finally agreed to meet him at the Waterloo Hotel where Donna and I went on Friday Nights. Donna and I were dancing round enjoying ourselves when Potter arrived. Potter came up behind Donna grabbed her arm (which was around me) and nearly broke it in an arm lock. Then he realized she was a female and let go. Donna was an African American, you see and she chose to wear suits and a tie. Potter was majorly embarrassed, I was horrified and Donna was ready to bash him.

This took the end of the relationship a step further because of course after that little incident Donna wouldn't have him at her flat at all.

It was around the same time my friend Tracey rang me at work and told me Ned was in town, Brisbane Town. Back from where ever it was he went to. Puckapunyal I think. Oh wow. I'd always had 'im in the back of my mind and on this day I decided to get all my stuff out of Donna's place and get a little piece of privacy of my very own. It just so happened, my boss at the Australian Archives had a vacant flat below his and it was only $60 a week. Smashing. I used to work for Australian Archives before I got dumped into the Tax Department. I really liked that job too, it was the best job I ever had, but unfortunately it was only a 16week temporary position, which lasted nearly three years in the end. The boss fancied me you see, so he just kept writing to Canberra and saying, we were flat out and still needed Nicky.

My little flat was really unique, with a raised kitchen and a sunken lounge, 2 bedrooms, one, which was actually useable, and the other was really just a storage room because it was on a steep slope, as was the whole place. It was a really good feeling having my own flat. No one could boss me round any more, no one could tell me where to go, or when to come home. This would be great. If I walked out that door I would have no time limit on when I came back again. Excellent!

As it happens, I always tend to follow my heart and not my head, Following my head would've made me richer, but only in money. At this particular time my heart was following Ned Kelly. So off I went into town to find the love of my life. This is him. HIM. I found the lovely bloke too, opposite Tracey at Lennons Plaza just where I expected to find him. We partied hard for the next few hours. I was very happy with this bloke, so what the hell, I took him home. He was easy, he was enjoyable and he was mine.

As per usual I was the only one who was **wrong.** He apparently took off the next day back to Puckapunyal where he had come from to do a 3-day course, something to do with Helicopters. I found all this out over the next few days, by ringing the Army barracks. I felt like I'd been used. I guess I shouldn't have because I really enjoyed myself, but it was just that I know he wasn't in pain like I was after the fact. He'd obviously gone back to the woman and child, again. I tried to track him down so I could just talk to him but never had any luck there.

Life goes on and work goes on, and we all have to get up in the morning. So work just filled my days and nothing much but the tely filled the lonely nights. Because I'm not a slut, (as far as I'm concerned) I couldn't bring just anyone home so ended up in the same bed with darling Potter again. Well it wasn't really the same bed, it was his bed or my bed. None of this really matters though because **we ended up pregnant.**

I invited him to lunch to tell him and he said he would stand by me whatever my decision. My decision was fairly unstable for at least the next month or so. (sorry Stu) It's just what we go through when there **are choices.** If we didn't have the choice then there would be no confusion for us poor Women. Undoubtedly it was a bloke who thought up the concept of abortion and it's also the blokes who line up outside the abortion clinics to harass the poor confused women or girls with the big signs with the words Murderer on them. Bastards. Bloody Bastards.

Anyway after a fair bit of mind-boggling bullshit I woke up to myself and remembered that all I ever wanted my whole life, was children. When I was a little girl I had my whole bed full of baby dolls and I was always hanging off the edge of the bed. I had to smack myself in the face this time and continue on. *Because life goes on, ya know, ya know it ain't easy, you've just gotta be strong, because we're all, part of the sixties.*

I think everyone else around, except for me, thought—this means on goes the wedding. Well you can't take back what happened yesterday, you can't suddenly be in love if you weren't yesterday; you can't say "Till death do us part" if it's not really in your heart. You can let someone look after you though, for a while. You can try to give them what they want, for a while. You can share the bonding (or not) of the screaming lump of flesh, mentioned earlier, but nothing can ever change your heart.

I stayed in my lovely little flat for a few more months and continued to work in the Tax Department, and then Potter got transferred to Mt Isa of all places. OK so if I'm doing this I'll obviously have to go with him. It may have been at Potter's own request, not sure on that one and probably never will be.

It was all new to me. New places, new faces and this tiny little person growing inside me. I was happy. I got right into it for a while, babies and baby books, knitting and sewing, quilting and making all sorts for my growing belly, but in the forty-degree heat who really cares. I clearly remember one day up there I sat at the Mt Isa Hospital for about five hours and then I got the complete shits and rang Potter at work! He came. I was so upset and hot and emotional by then I just cried in his arms when he finally got there. The stupid people at the counter had put my chart in the "Out Tray". Oh my God, no one, well no male anyway, can quite understand what we go through. All I wanted to do was go home and I didn't really know where home was anymore. Potter just thought I was bloody stupid, and I felt bloody stupid as well.

As I got fatter and fatter it seemed to get hotter and hotter, and Potter seemed to care less and less. I wonder if this sounds familiar to anyone at all. It should have been the most wonderful time of my life, but it was not. I was so so sad. And so alone. Potter went to work each day and started to stay on after work for the odd beer, with mates. This was not his usual caper but what did he have to come home to. ME. Our relationship wasn't much chop before this pregnancy bit, so how could it possibly get any better. I tried, maybe.

The next thing to change the scenery was a weekend away, with the computer boys from the mines. It was a camping trip out to the back of beyond. Mary Cathrine, I think was the name of the place and I don't think it exists any more either. Yahoo! Something is actually happening in my life other than sitting in a hot box of a flat all day, getting fatter. I hadn't met any of Potter's work mates or their wives before. P'raps he's ashamed of me. (probably still is) Ya get that.

After a couple of hours drive, we arrived at some old pub. Right in the middle of nowhere, it was. It was a funny little set up, just one pub surrounded by half a dozen houses, and that was it. Christ knows what would possess anyone to want to go there, let alone live there. Whatever else happened that day, I was going to enjoy myself. After a few hours at this aforementioned pub, one of those with more cobwebs than styles of beer, grief struck once again, to this ever-so-thrilling relationship.

It came in the form of a jealous green giant. It was so bloody stupid too. Potter and I had been sitting at a table with some local bloke for about an hour chatting about kids and babies and stuff. He had a wife and a six-week-old baby at home. We could probably all get together some time in the future to play cards or something was what the conversation was about. I went to the loo. The bloke went to the loo. It was way out the back. You know the sort. One of those dunnys with a red back on the toilet seat. As I came out so did the bloke. He held my two hands in his and said, "Gee it's nice to meet such nice people a way out here."

Potter came out of nowhere and said, "What's going on here"?

He ripped my hands away as he said it and my mouth got the better of me as per usual.

"We're just having a quick fuck, what does it look like?"

I was promptly dragged off and then out to the car. Most of the other work fellas were leaving as well so this was the end of a good day. When we got back to the campsite, everyone else was sitting around a campfire in a long dried up riverbed. I got out of the car to go and join everyone and Potter grabbed me and pushed me to the ground. He had my arm twisted up behind my back nearly breaking it, and he also had his hand over my mouth to stop me from screaming. Unfortunately his hand was also over my nose. I struggled and struggled to get away. I didn't want to scream any more I just wanted to breathe. I'm sure the tiny baby inside me wanted to breathe as well. I could not believe he was doing this. I couldn't believe he'd still hurt me while I was carrying his child. Some couple walked by, thank Christ and said, "Are you OK?."

Potter let go immediately and I said, "No I'm not OK, I'll probably never be OK again."

I got up and went down to join the rest of the folk round the fire. I spent the rest of the night crying on some body's shoulder. What should have been a lovely night had turned into a horror show for me. I knew I could not forgive Potter for this. I slept in the tent we had put up earlier and in the morning Potter had gone. I had to hitch a lift, well me and my belly, the three fucking hour drive back to The Isa. Great thinking, Potter. Needless to say he was the sorriest fucker alive by the time I finally arrived back to the little hot box that we called home. All I wanted then from him was a bus ticket home. Wherever that was. Three long weeks later he finally bought me the ticket I wanted and I got on that bus. I'm crying now just writing about this, but I can only try to describe how I felt as I got on that bus. Lost, alone, grief stricken, broken hearted just complete and utter despair

Off on the bus with my heart in my mouth, (mainly because the growing baby was taking up all the room) back to Brisbane. To my sister's house. I got harassed on the bus by some male specimen, who wanted to share my blanket. He saw me get on the bus bawling my eyes out, obviously pregnant and still he attempted to be a leach and leper while the 22-year-old pregnant bitch slept. He got an awful shock when I woke up though because I smacked him in the mouth and pissed him off to another seat, other than that I'd have him thrown off all together.

Another day later I got out of that bus outside the Kedron Park Hotel, Lutwyche. I thought I'd surprise Lyns Bag and just walk to their place, but after I got as far as the phone I decided to ring would be much easier. Kellie came to pick me up about ten minutes later. Good ol' Kellie. I felt at home already just being around her. Considering the way I felt all these wonderful people in Malinda's place made me feel a lot better—almost at home. Home away from home. ***Where-ever I lay my hat that's my home.*** Home is where the heart is. Actually it was an extreme contrast to the way I was living the day before.

The household consisted of my big sister, Kellie, Mary, and two very ordinary blokes, and who gives a rats about their names and now me as well and my rather protruding belly. I remember that day like it was yesterday and I remember another day as an outstanding one of my past.

Here was I, eight and a half months pregnant and Potters' Mum and my Mum were coming for luncheon as it were. At least I'd got over meeting her before being pregnant, that can turn out pretty handy as mothers-in-law go. They don't fancy it to much meeting their prospective daughter-in-law when she is about to turn them into a Grandparent, can't blame them I s'pose.

Lyns and I made scones, Kellie was out at work and I think Mary was trying to sleep. The "first time Grandmas" arrived, seconds after the Social Security had arrived to check out Kelly and her son and their circumstances. Also, before that Atlas had arrived and there were a couple of extra's downstairs playing pool. My Mum of course brought her dog as always she has and there was another young lass that lobbed in with her small dog.

As the scones and tea came out, so did Atlas who entered, sculled half a litre of milk, belched loudly and with a "How ya's going Grandmas" and away out the other exit. Next the two dogs were going in and out chasing each other through the legs and the chair legs. All the while there were shrieks of laughter coming from down below and then in walked a couple of bikers to put a six pack or two in the fridge, "Excuse us Love."

I continued on trying to be Hostess with the mostess and whether I failed or not no longer mattered to me. I wanted to assure the other grandma her son's child would be looked after, regardless of the way things worked out. I think all things considered that I failed miserably.

I knew I could not stay here and have a baby in this sort of lifestyle and with all these other people around me. I really didn't mix with them at all in that month or so that I stayed there, except a few rare occasions. Memorable occasions at that. Like the night we played sculls or 7's as they sometimes call it. If you get it wrong you scull, whatever it is your drinking, which happened to be cask wine. I played too by the way, but I had a different level that I filled my glass up to. It ended up quite a sick night, literally. A few people ended up hanging over the bath edge spewing, and then finally in the bath still spewing. I won't mention any names.

I started looking for a flat of my own again, the cheaper the better. Potter had been sending flowers every Friday for the past 4 weeks and a tape along with it saying how sorry he was (for himself). Anything had to be better than this mayhem. I was still pretty young and naive and stupid but still I knew this is definitely not where my baby is starting out life. NO WAY!

I found my 2nd home that, I found and I decided on, and it was mine, my place, the nest for me and mine. I was scared though about the inevitable birth. I really needed someone to hold my hand. That's how it's s'posed to be after all. *We can work it out. We can work it out.* Who was I trying to kid, obviously not myself.

Potter got a transfer back from Mt Isa to Brissy. He had three weeks holiday before returning to work. In the first week he moved into the horrible little dump I'd picked out for us. The second week I went through the birth of my first child. I really wanted and needed that hand to grip and squeeze during labour. You know—someone to scream at and swear at and someone to BLAME for all this pain, I'm going through. I had that at least. I had it each and every time and for this, at least, I must be grateful and consider myself one of the luckier ones. The third week I was home and we were now a family. Potter and I took our new little son everywhere. It was a pretty happy time. Stuart Potter McFarlane was the first Grandson on either side. Oh what a little Darling he was. A son. A Boy. It's a Boy. He was perfect. He was born with the most perfect little features. Not like other babies with lumps and bumps and purple faces and squished up eyes, he was just absolutely perfect. A little china doll. This was my dream come true. It's a pity it wasn't Potter's as well.

He just wasn't ready. He bought nothing for the child or me. A pram is a Luxury he said. A jolly-jumper is definitely going too far. We had the nappies and a car seat though because his Mother had donated them and I had bought a few clothes and things during my stay at the MadHouse. I still had my maternity money though then so I at least had some dignity and some independence. That's all over. I'm Potters' Woman now and I never had a cent to my name. He was earning about $600 a week way back then in 1984 but I never had a cent in my pocket. We must remember after all that I'm an alcoholic and if I had any money I'd undoubtedly drink the lot and fall down with the baby!

Potter thought nothing of buying R.M. Williams boots at $200 a whack, bike magazines, new records every other day and Perry Cardigan Ties, etc etc. I couldn't even have a fucking pram. Well, my big sis came through for me again. She was working in Sydney by this time and she used to send me $100 a fortnight to survive on, so life was looking up for me and I dashed out and bought a pram and a Jolly-Jumper immediately. The following fortnight I got a high chair, which also converted, to a swing.

A few more weeks and it was back to the Tax Department for me and I must say I was glad. Not to leave my precious child but to have some money again. My own money in my own bleedin' pocket. There was a lady living in the downstairs flat who was to baby-sit my little Stuey. I was only doing this for six months to save enough for a deposit on our own house. Six months and I'm home again with my little baby boy.

Potter was working late a fair bit at this time. We were also fighting a fair bit. He was s'posed to pick me up after work one particular evening and I waited and waited on the corner near the Tax Department for nearly an hour and then I rang his work. They told me he had left a couple of hours earlier, so I knew he had no intention what so ever of picking me up at all. I rang the babysitter and organized her for the night. Then I went back to work and found a girlfriend to party with.

After a few hours of drinking and dancing my friend, her mate, and I all went back to my place about midnight and Potter was home by then. I woke him up and yelled, "What the fuck happened to you. You promised to pick me up around 5pm and you left work at 4pm" I was pissed off yes, and I was angry, bloody angry. I was shaking him by the shoulders to wake him up but I still don't feel I deserved what I got next. He suddenly leapt up and punched me off the bed but that wasn't enough. I was still lying on the bedroom floor holding my face and crying when he got on top of me went for it again and again, then he calmly got back in to bed.

After a few minutes I got up and all I could feel was hate. I went to the kitchen and got out the biggest (always the biggest) knife and ran back up the hallway. Carol and her mate stopped me and got the knife out of the way and calmed me down again. The three of us slept on the lounge room floor then. I didn't sleep though, not for ages. Everything was swimming round and round in my head. I had to go get my son in a few hours—I've got to go to work as well in the morning. Well morning did come and I woke to Potter packing his stereo and TV up just at the end of my feet. He left for work shortly after I woke and said, "I'll be back to get all my shit at the weekend," and with that he slammed the door and left. ***"Thanks for your time and you can thank me for mine, and after that's said forget it!***

So I went down and got my little Stuey and came back upstairs and sat in my lonely little flat and cried. I cried and cried. I looked at Stuey and cried. I bathed him and dressed him and cried, I fed him and cried some more. I didn't think my face and eyes could puff up anymore but I looked in the mirror and cried even more and even louder. Who I was crying for, of course, was not positive, maybe myself and maybe for the small innocent child sitting on my lap, I think probably both.

Finally I stopped sniveling and feeling sorry for my silly self and took in deep breaths and blew them out again, slowly and determinedly. In and out in and out. Right then, what next. I had a few big decisions to make here. What to do, what to do. Well what do I mostly want. What was it I had wanted or maybe expected from wonderful daddy the first. What I wanted always, was Mr. Right and six kids, well I got the first bit wrong and now I have this beautiful blonde haired blue eyed boy in front of me, so it's for him I can go on. What I had expected was a home of my own. Well it would not ever have been mine so now I'll have to do it alone. I can and I bloody well will. I'll show him.

I will show him, you just watch me.

ME, MYSELF & I

I finished up with the Tax Department once more. This time forever. I quit this time so's I could get my superannuation. As it happens I got nearly 4,000 bucks. I wanted to buy a house and put a roof over my son's head, as a parent should. I rang Dad and said, "Stop right there Dad, how much do you want for the Island house, as is."

We had a holiday house on Macleay for years and now that Ma and Pa had moved over there and into their new beachfront home, the first place was vacant. Dad was doing it up to sell. He did NOT want to sell it to me under any circumstances. Not with all the bodgy jobs that had been done to it over the years. "How much Dad" I repeated.

Once he realized I was serious, he helped me in every way possible. I had to go for a Housing Commission Loan first. Dad and I went to see them on the Tuesday and the Receptionist said there's an appointment vacant in about six months, or there's been a cancellation today and you could get in at 3.00pm. I already had every item they could possibly ask for, like Tax Records, Bank Statements, Birth Certificate etc. etc. so we took the 3.00pm interview. The Ball was rolling. I got Dad's Solicitor for all the legal bullshit and I got the first home buyers Grant for $7,000, and within one month I had an approved loan with the Housing Commission and my own HOME.

I'll never forget that day, I was so happy and so damn proud of myself. I'm just so clever and I got my own home now, na na, na na na! All I wanted to do as usual was to celebrate. Yahoo! I rang Potter's Mum to see if she could baby-sit for me. No problem. The next problem was where to go and who to go with. I rang a few mates who were already out. My girlfriend from Australian Archives was going to the Kedron Wavell R.S.L. for dinner, a quiet dinner, just her and her fellow. I explained to her that I'd just got the loan through for my first house and wanted to celebrate and that I only needed someone to go with and then I'd get out of her face. Bob and Debbie picked me up about an hour later and off we went to the R.S.L. They went upstairs to dine and I went downstairs to the poolroom. Well what a night! A few beers later and a game of pool occurs, two girls and two guys. We won of course—but undoubtedly they let us.

CHAPPIE 7

LOZZA

Well he pinched my arse after the 2nd game of pool together. I said "Hey you just pinched my arse you cheeky bastard." He said, "You didn't mind though, did you?" "Oh not really" I replied.

We partied a few hours at the R.S.L. and then off to the valley by cab. MMMM, must have a few dollars this Lad, not that I ever really cared and I did quite fancy him. To me he was a man, a real man. How did I know that, I didn't, but he was ten years older than I was so he must be. Lozza was his name. Gorgeous eyes, gorgeous skin, a happy go lucky type bloke, Ahhh! I think it's love at first sight NO! I was just so deliriously happy about getting a home for me and mine. He thought I was drunk the first moment he met me, but this was not the case. It was a feeling of power, elation. I had won the last test and I could stand on my own two feet now. I was someone and not just someone's woman.

Back to the story. Lozza took me to this illegal card joint, upstairs somewhere in Fortitude Valley, I think it was above Tony's' Bar, couldn't be sure. I had a bloody good time I know that much. It was free drinks for me the whole time, anything I wanted while Lozza was gambling. I didn't really notice what he was doing anyway, I was just enjoying myself as usual. He took me home to his place in the end. I wouldn't have known where my place was anyway by then—so it was probably for the best. I'm sure he thought so until . . . . Whoops! Woke up with a wet bed.

I was so embarrassed. This was the first time. It was a waterbed too so it spreads right out. But you of course could blame it on the bed. I cleaned it up and washed the sheets. Lozza sat in the lounge and watched the sports. I was so stupid in those days. I rang my girlfriend Debbie and asked her to please pick me up. To this Lozza yelled out, "oh no, stay for the day and I'll drive you home tomorrow,"(Which means wouldn't mind another fuck—now that I know) I was so wrapped when he said that. I said my sorry's to Deb for waking her up and told her I'd been asked to stay.

I met his two Kids that day. A girl and boy, about 11 and 12 years old. Great kids, good-looking kids, but what do you do with them. I only just learnt about constipation in infants and how to sort that out and I could easily make up a bottle and change a nappy but they didn't need either. We all got on all right though and I think Lozza needed me there, more than I needed to be there. If you can understand that. He didn't seem even slightly bothered about the wet bed scene and it was never mentioned. He did drive me home that next day, back to my little flat, the one I was so happy to get only a few months earlier. Things change though and how.

I never thought I'd see young Lozza again, because of the bed-wetting incident but about a week later he arrived. My mate and me were having a smoke at the time and had to get rid of it. "Shit, shit, shit, get rid of it quick," I'm running round like a lunatic trying to hide the pot and spray the place as well. Shit, Lozza is a Customs Agent, and we had to get rid of it, you know the caper. After Lozza had been there for awhile and I'd got to know him better, he explained the difference between Customs Officer and a Customs Agent. Then we had another smoke.

I really don't remember the next bit of my life. I've never actually thought about it till writing this bleedin' book—but I do not remember packing, I don't remember getting myself or Stuart or any of our stuff from the little flat to the New House on Macleay Island. I know I had a Hillman on the Mainland, which I'd bought off Debbie, and I know I had the same Hillman on the Island. I also know that Stuart and I got over there too but how? None of the furniture was the same because it wasn't MINE. I had no records because I wouldn't have bought any in the last three years. I believe I had nothing but the Fucking Hillman and the House and Stuey and they were **MINE, *mine, mine, mine all mine. It should be mine, mine mine; mine all mine.***

I got a bankcard then so I could furnish the house. One thousand dollars to furnish the Homestead and it's amazing what you can do with 1,000 bucks. You could spend it all easily on fast cars and flashy women, but you could also buy:—a washing machine, fridge, freezer, lounge suite, bedroom suite, crockery cutlery and a *partridge and a pear tree*. Let me tell you it was all a bit daggy but was all mine.

So I guess the wall was built right back then. A wall between me and a real man, because I'd done his job now. Well I had to. We can't all sit around feeling sorry for ourselves and dye our hair blonde to go with the brains they think we've got. They, being men, of course. Once you've made step one and bought a house, you also have to follow it up with the home maintenance plan as well. Gutters, plumbing, mowing and mowers, water tanks and water pumps, gas and gas fittings, electric fuses and on and on it goes.

I didn't mind learning all these things and as you may remember my Dad was a jack of all trades and master of most. He helped me with all these sorts of things most of the time, I s'pose he could see no one else was gonna!

Lozza was a businessman and a Ladies man and that's where it ended. I used to drive my shit box car up to his place on a Friday afternoon do a spot of cleaning up and put some sort of dinner on and then make myself **beautiful** and wait for my Darling Lozza to come home. After awhile it got to being Thursday that I'd go dashing up to his place and Monday or Tuesday that I'd return to my home to Macleay. He never actually asked me to Marry him but he did ask me to move in with him permanently. I sort of did, but the days just changed around and I stayed at Lozza's' all week and went home on the weekend just to mow the lawns and make the place look lived in. I was still on a single pension, and was not willing to give this up, not after the way Potter had made me feel about myself and about what I was worth, which was nothing.

After about a year or so of his non caring behavior I realized my house was starting to deteriorate and I was forever cleaning up at Lozza's rented home. He had an in-ground pool too, which was a lot of work. I had to keep the gardens nice as well, because he had an inspection every three months. It was quite a busy time for me. I had 2 homes to keep, my baby Stuey and Lozza's two kids as well. I was also his receptionist for the next year or so because he started his own Custom Agency and was working from home. I also realized I was doing absolutely everything for him and he was doing absolutely fuck-all for me. At this point I started to go home more often and he did not follow. Not even on the weekends. He couldn't have lived with me because of his work, I understood this fact, but he still didn't come over on the weekends never or very rarely. Then he started looking for a boarder to help him pay the rent. As it turned out my sister was returning from down Sydney way, so I lined her up to take a room at Lozza's. At least this way she could keep an eye on him for me. Then I started to get jealous each time I went up to Lozza's. I started to wonder about the two of them. They seemed to have more in common. They used to go to the Gym together, twice a week and to the R.S.L. to play pool and stuff. I was beside myself. I really didn't know what to do or what to say. If I said anything at Lozza's I was just a Jealous Idiot, and I should shut the fuck up. What's new?

After a few months I got the shits with the whole deal. His excuses for why he couldn't come to the Island each time and the whole shebang! I told him it was over and I'm sick to death of you and the whole relationship, and Goodbye!

My girlfriend, Kellie said, "Oh I'm so glad you've done that, now I can tell ya!

"Tell me what,:" I Yelled
"Tell you about your sister and Lozza."
"What!" I yelled even louder.

My next move was to leave the Island right here and right now. I just wanna kill someone.

"Well they were coming down the Island about six months ago to tell you that they'd fallen in love and they're Sorry."

"I'll give them fucking sorry."

Malinda had previously told Kelly at the Redland Bay Hotel when they were all coming over together. She had also said that she woke up in his bed and was surrounded by flowers, roses at that.

Well I never, no I never got any bloody flowers, least of all roses. No wonder Lyns had been so anti-**Lozza** for the past few months, calling him a bastard and saying I should dump him.

Right! Well someone or other has to be bashed over this. Maybe two someone or others.

"You're babysitting Kellie, and I'm off to the Mainland to get my revenge" I crashed my Suzuki 70 step-thru into the jetty shed and jumped up and ran down the jetty to catch the last boat. I was bawling by this time and had also seriously scraped my knees and elbows.

My favorite Skipper, Tim, (who was born in the double U's) was concerned about my state and asked me what was wrong. "I've just found out my MAN (HUH) is playing around on me and that my gut feelings were right all along, and I'm going to kill someone. I leapt into the old Hillman revved the shit out of it and took off in a cloud of dust to find those who had hurt me. Oh I'll just slip into the Reddy Bay for a couple of bottles of strongbow and then away! Must get our priorities right, liquid courage first, bashing second.

Well somehow I managed to drive and slurp myself all the way from the Redland Bay to Chermside once again. I got up to the house and no bastard was there. I ran crazily through the house that I'd been cleaning for the last two years, looking for clues. Who needs clues, stupid bitch. They're out together right now. While I'm going crazy wondering if it's really true—stupid bitch again.

And I'm also about to stab Lozza's' waterbed to death, when a car pulls up. It's Malinda and guess who's driving, NO, you're wrong, it's not Lozza at all it's P.P. Who's P.P. you may ask? You'll find the answer in the 6th chappie. Oh my good God! Oh my God! Potter saw the threatening look and scarpered real quick—after all he's seen this shit before.

Lyns got up the stairs and I swung a good right hook, pity I missed though and fell over, then she kicked me in the guts a few times— yelling the same obscenities to me as I was just yelling at her. Slut, Bitch, Tart, Trollop, just to name a few. By the time I picked my drunken idiot self up off the verandah floor, she had dived into her room and shoved something against the door, possibly a wardrobe or two. I yelled a lot more and was banging on doors and walls a bit. You know, like a complete crazy and then another car pulled up. It was Lozza this time and a few of his mates. Lozza came up alone. I came unexpectedly out of the kitchen and slapped him straight in the face.

"Why? Why? Malinda. You Fuckin' Bastard." The sheer innocence that came from those eyes.

He said, "Hang on a minute Nick, just let me go tell my mates I'm not coming and we'll sort this out.

He convinced me with his usual style that nothing had happened, and all he said was true. Lyns Bags meant nothing to him at all and he loved me and only me. I was his girl. I was the only one. I was such an idiot at the time with this sort of thing, I actually believed him. Well not really, but I guess we do this shit to ourselves for some reason. I loved him. I loved him yesterday so there fore I'll love him today and possibly tomorrow. I thought so anyway, but it didn't take long to wear off after that.

I did continue on with him for about 6 months after that, but it was never the same, if you know what I mean. I went up to his place less and less. The Island was my home now. I felt so anyway. I went up to Brisbane to see another close friend of mine who'd been going out with Lozza's best mate and she had thought It was over with for months anyway. She showed me photos of a recent party with another Tax Department friend sitting, rather snugly on Lozza's lap. She also told me that in the morning when she was cleaning up, she had found them in the 69er position in her spare room and she hadn't realized anyone was still in the house. I felt so stupid and so used but it really didn't hurt like before. **It was over. It was over in my heart.**

Goodbye to you it's hard to cry, when all the birds
are singing in the sky,
I tried to know what's right from wrong and
now it's time to move along.

CHAPPIE 8

FAT GAZZ

This particular fellow was actually waiting on the jetty for me, when I arrived back there with all the stuff that had piled up at Lozza's. You'd never believe it of course unless you were there. Which I was, with young Stuart and his playpen and pram and all that shit. I had met him a few times on the Island at different parties and I knew he fancied me and here he was. He knew immediately that the relationship on the Mainland was over. I was 24ish and still the same naive idiot I was years before, **STILL. But here I was alone again, I hate that.** Gazza offered me a hand with all my gear and I naturally accepted. I wanted to party as usual, just a few drinks to get over the last Bastard. **He was more than willing to come round for a few.**

He was a bearded wonder. A long bushy red beard and no hair on top at all, with long ringlets protruding out each side of the cap that I'd never seen him without. I guess he was trying to make up for his loss on top. **Fat Gazz was his name, bullshitting to anyone was his game.** But at the time he was a crutch for me in between blokes. **Ha. Ha.** Honestly, when I met him I thought he was such a great guy. A great big, happy helper. A gentle giant. He was almost as round as he was tall and I could barely get my arms around him.

Week one and he was absolutely wonderful to me and to Stuart. He helped round the house when he came over. He took us out to the pub a few times and he shouted as well. He professed his love to me a dozen times a day, and I believed he really did love me. He wasn't the sort to be a womanizer either. I was the only one for him and he'd known it for a long time. He was so glad that I'd finally split with Lozza so he could have his chance (his way).

I can't actually place the particular time we got engaged, but it was only after a few weeks at the most. He didn't ask on bended knee either, mainly because he couldn't bend his knees. I was really happy with him and he was madly in love with me. I was having a bloody good time as per, and after another few weeks he moved in. He moved in to my house. I should've asked myself then—why doesn't this man have his own house? He's older than me and he's got nothing. I didn't though, I was just enjoying myself. Nothing changes. He brought all his worldly belongings with him, which were made up of 1 doona and 1 dog. **What an input. What a champion.** As you can plainly see, love is blind, and it certainly doesn't help if you're blind as well. It's just a shame, once again, that it wasn't love at all. It was just a big, fat, user who had nothing to do and nowhere better to go.

Another month or so went by and I started to see the real Gazz. He got some smoko off his best mate. The mate he'd been living with and who had also recently taken him to Bali for a holiday completely at his own cost. When his mate showed up to get the money off Gazz on the said day, Gazz told him he'd been busted and the cops got the lot and that he also had a large fine. I knew it was all bullshit because I had smoked some of it myself with Gazz. I didn't know what to say, so I just said nothing at all. I couldn't believe he'd do this to his best mate. He was obviously a complete arsehole. He also started to get funny with me about where I was going and when I'd be back etc. HUH! Then he even got funny with Stuart, saying things like, **"I don't think that he should associate with our kids when we have some." How disgusting is that?**

Needless to say the relationship didn't last very long after that. I still had to be the one to go though. Leave your own house for a while Naughty Nickers, maybe he'll fuck off then. He just wouldn't leave you see. Hey, I really did give it a go to start with, but I was getting the bad end of the stick as usual. When he first moved in you see, the Social Security came over to see me one day and I wasn't there so Gazza had told them he lived there and that we were getting married. Naturally they cut me off the single pension and I got a job immediately. I went up to Golden Cockerel, which was about 10kms from the Mainland jetty, and got on the first day. Gazz was dropping me off at work and apparently looking for work after that. I started at 6am so he was plenty early enough to find work, especially as he was a brick layer. Well, guess what? He was just driving my car round all day and visiting my mates from day to day and smoking pot with them and drinking our money away. Sometimes he never even bothered to pick me up.

Here I was paying all the bills, house, gas, electricity, phone and a babysitter for young Stuart, and working my arse off all day as well, while this **lazy fat bastard was putting in absolutely jack shit.**

After staying a week or so at my friend Sue's place on the Mainland I finally went home and he was gone. He had left his dog though and his doona, so I still scored something, didn't I. Oh lucky me! Some chicks apparently get rings and cars and stuff, even houses; me, I got the dog.

He did come back a few days later and I fucked off again up to Sandy's place this time. (one of my ol' drinking buddies) He came up and found me there too. When the male or Ex-male does this and doesn't seem to quite get the picture, one has no choice but to tell the truth the whole truth and nothing but the truth. So I gave it to him good and proper. **"Well Gazz, I thought you were a big happy, jolly, easy going, gentle giant who'd look after me and my young son, BUT you're really a big, fat, lazy, good for nothing, lying cunt who thinks of no-one but himself. Furthermore you** couldn't even support a family if your poor old mother did actually die and leave you all her money, which is all you're waiting for and FUCK OFF!" He finally left.

Sandy and I had a few celebratory drinks and then I went home alone once more. *Goodbye Gazz, thanks for coming.*

THE CHAPPIE OF ALL CHAPPIES

Well believe it or not I had learnt something by now, in fact I knew it all. Dad could have told any of them that years before. I will not be told anything and I can do it all by myself. Dad also said to me on many occasions, that no one will ever look after me, because of this very reason. Men like dopey, silly blondes that they can take care of and also tell what to do. Not this kid though, I could never be told what to do not even by my Father, well not after 18 anyway.

By now I knew all the types of blokes that I would have to contend with, **the violent, the cheaters, the liars and the leavers and not to mention the Clingons, (not the sort that Dr, Spock had to deal with) and last but not least the Fathers who could do all of the above.** I'm ready now for anything and no one can use or abuse me anymore, because I've got it all and I've done it all and it's all mine.

I was still working at the Chicken Factory, paying off my house and enjoying life as it happened. The car shit itself—what's new, and I was walking 2kms every morning on a backwards run to the

Babysitters with young Stuart. Then it was about 7 kms to the jetty for work, but I left early enough to get Stuart to Big Barbs and then hitch to the jetty. Everyone knew everyone in those days on Macleay, so as long as I left enough time to be jetty bound before the 6.08 boat, I knew I'd get there. Oh what a keen worker. That was probably the only good thing the last bloke did, and that was to get me back into the work force, it makes you feel better about yourself, even if you're just a drunk. Which I really wasn't, way back then.

I walked the hitch-hiker's path up and down that Island for a few months after the **Hillman died.** I didn't mind it though. Well not after awhile anyway and after I'd lost a few chunks of excess lard, the walk got quicker and easier and I could leave a bit later. After I'd lost about two stone, which I'm still unsure what it is in kilos; I was spotted! P'raps I was spotted by quite a few, but I never really noticed. I just wanted to drink and party, meet new people, play darts, pool, cards and just generally have a fucking good time. I would not be told when to come home or why, and when I was ready to go home, I left, usually alone in my shit box car (when it went) and usually with Stuart. Shock! Horror!

We always got home—but that's obvious. One night when I got home with young Stuart there was a King Brown wandering up my bedroom wall in the corner of the room. I had to back off slowly from the big bastard and get next door to grab Stuart out of his bed and then run through the long grass and then down a couple of streets on an unmoonlit evening. I ran and ran (fuck all the snakes in the long grass). When I got to my mate's place, no one was home or just not answering. I kept going up the street to another mate's place. There was half a party going on at Trevor's place, a few blokes and a couple of chicks. When I told them my problem they all laughed at me.

Men will be men and boys will be boys and they decided it was just a carpet snake. So off they went, led by my mate Trevor to hunt the killer python. I had a great time with all the young chicky babes, and I s'pose at the time I really wasn't much older myself. I think we enjoyed each other's company for an hour or so and then. Da Da da da!

They arrived back with the head of a King Brown.

Ha Ha! The laugh was on them. Apparently it gave them a run for their money. Stuart and I finally went home once the coast was clear. It was always at these unfortunate times, that I really so much wished I had a man of my own, to help out with life's little dramas. I was really getting sick of doing it all by myself and to be honest, I really can't do it all.

I was going on 26 by now and Stu' was nearly 4, we had our own house and two cars now, one for the Island and another for the Mainland. As far as I was concerned, this was not what I'd expected to achieve for myself by this ripe old age.

Then one night after one of my many little piss ups at home, all of my mates had left and I wasn't quite ready to finish up yet. The night was still young. Off I go down the road with me big, black dog, to continue the night elsewhere. It's only about 1km away if I cut across the neighbour's place at the end of my street. As I walked through their yard, the dogs started going off their brains, because of my dog. So I got just past the back verandah and this large bloke flies out in mid air to karate kick me in the head.

'It's only me,' I yelled out in despair. He must have heard a woman's' voice and he stopped himself from kicking me and fell to the ground and I tripped over him anyway and we fell into as mound. He said he was terribly sorry but the previous night and the night before someone had been siphoning petrol from his and his brother-in-law's cars. That was the night I first met what was to be the father of my 2nd child. Interesting way of meeting, hey!

Well a day or two later the same fellow gave me and my much smaller arse a lift home. Isn't it amazing, after all this time, one can be noticed for one's flaming body and nothing else. **HUH!** But on the same token I thought, **WOW, what a body he had—best I've seen in a long time and really good looking as well.** Dark skinned, 6ft at the very least and just gorgeous. **Handsome is as handsome**

does, so the saying goes. He was lovely though and he took me all the way up to pick up Stuart and then dropped me off to my door. What a champ! Another few days went by and I ran into him again with his brother-in-law at the local dealer's place. The two of them bought their stick, or whatever and left and I did the same.

The very next evening the two fellows knocked on my own back door, "Hi Nick, just wondering whether or not you have any pot left." Naturally I did have, because I'm really a drinker and not so much a smoker. I also just happened to have half a carton in the fridge as well, so I invited them both in. They stayed awhile and we got to know each other a bit, which was really lovely as far as I was concerned. Jarmas, the good looking one, had just moved up here from Bendigo, and was staying in the house at the end of my street with his Sister Kaz and Spring Head, how fortunate.

The next meeting was down at Kazzas when she looked after Stuart for the day. After work I called in to pick him up and Kaz asked me in for a drink. I was more than happy to do this in the hopes that Jarmas would return while I was there. He did, which was natural enough, after all he did live there. So I got to see Mr. Good Looking once again. This time I got pretty pissy (an unusual state of affairs) and when Jarmas offered me a lift home I jumped at the chance. When we got to my back door I invited him in, of all things, what a complete bag. I expected him to take the opportunity—like any male, but he said, "You don't really want that Nicky, you're just drunk." To which I replied, "Yes you're right, I am pretty drunk, Goodnight."

I was really a lot more than just drunk, I was bloody lonely and wanted a man to come along and sweep me off my feet and make mad passionate love to me. Well not tonight, sweetheart.

After that I saw him here and there and he also gave me the odd lift if he happened along. Then he seemed to be at the jetty on a regular basis to especially to give me a lift I guess. Finally after a few months from the first encounter of the most wonderful kind, we ended up in bed. I think they call it sex these days but to me it was love. I was also happy it had happened this way and not on the night I'd first offered my drunken self to him. He started giving me a lift in the mornings then as well, which was bloody marvelous. He was everything to me. He was funny as well as being romantic, manly, heroic and a bleedin' taxi driver, what more could one ask for?

He decided to come up to Golden Cockerel with me to hopefully get a job. In those days you just had to line up out the front and the boss would come out a pick whoever he needed from the crowd. The more often you were seen, the more likely it would be that the boss would pick you. I was lucky when I first started because I got picked the first day and then got put on Permanent Casual the second week. I am a bloody good worker though, even if I do say so myself.

Well Jarmas too, got on the first day. I'm sure I must have looked stunningly gorgeous to him with all my work clobber on. White uniform and white boots, hairnet and white cap over the top—no make-up, but who'd bother with it just to work in a chook factory. You'd be surprised. There were only about 10 men inside the factory and the rest worked outside on the docks or in the freezers. I thought I was a bit lucky here, because my MAN was put inside at the end of the line with me. Well me and about another 100 women, some of which wore a full set of make-up sexy stockings and leg warmers to match their earrings. Silly bitches, what a waste of time, and at 5.30 in the bloody morning.

Things went on happily for us little workers for quite awhile. We used to finish at all sorts of odd times of the day. This all depended on the Kill, which was between 20,000 and 50,000 in a day at that point in time. So more often than not we would just miss a boat home and end up at the Redland Bay Pub till the next one, or the one after that. After the initial taste of those few, we'd get a six pack for the old ferry trip, which took about a six pack. In normal language that's about 40mins. Then sometimes we'd even go to ol' Bill Brewster's for yet another one. (a six pack) Not to worry, we were young and we didn't get hang-overs. It was a happy, happy time.

Karen and Spring decided they wanted to move off the Island at this point. Karen always hated it anyway. So Mr Darling Jarmas asked me if he could move in because he wanted to keep his job and he wanted to keep me too. I naturally jumped at the idea, this is just what I wanted, wasn't it? As much as I really loved him, I still went into shock as he moved his stuff in. He hung a few paintings, moved a few things around and wanted space in a cupboard or two! Shit! **Fancy wanting space in a cupboard.**

I handled it though and Stuart was definitely wrapped. Jarmas was very good with kids and he was great with Stuey; after all, he did have two young nephews, one around the same age.

Things went on the same happy way, and then I found out I was pregnant—**Oh no. I wasn't ready.** I was happy like this. I was working. I was bloody **SLIM. I was not having a baby.—NOT NOW.** It's too soon. Jarmas said, **"You won't abort any child of mine, we'll get married."** That was obviously the end of that. Sounded like a fairly suitable idea. Well as it turned out, I wasn't pregnant after all, it was a **false alarm. Thank Christ!**

About 3 more months went by though and I really was **preggers this time,** No doubt about it. Well I really did love him and now that I'd had the extra time to get used to him, I decided that I was ready, I was more than ready. I was getting older and what better subject to have as a Father than the one I love.

This time Jarmas said, **"Here's $120.00 to go to the Clinic."** Well bugger me. I was flabbergasted. I threw the dollars at him and drove out of there like a maniac. He tried to stop me, but only managed to smash the driver's window instead. I kept going and went to me ol' mates' place, my neighbor and special friend, from Macleay Island. It's always good to talk things out, even if you've made up your mind, anyhow. So we're now at the point where Jarmas can go jump out of a flying plane and I will have this baby regardless of him or his support. I cried a lot, I remember that much. I couldn't understand what had happened in the past few months to change his whole attitude. After that we got together at home and spent a lot time talking about things. Jarmas explained that he thought that was what I wanted a few months earlier so he just gave the money over straight away. Things had changed. I really was pregnant this time and I intended to stay that way.

As I got fatter he seemed to flirt more and more with the girls at work. I should not have let it worry me, because I was carrying HIS child, but I could not help it. I was so jealous at this time and watched his every move, at work and at home. He did make me stress out even more though because he didn't want to make me feel loved and cared for and happy. He seemed to want me to witness him chatting up all the girls and the younger the better, even though he was only 3 years younger than me. Now that I think of it he's not all that bloody gorgeous anyway. He even used to wear his favourite jeans to work, which basically had no crotch in them. Now every chicky babe in the entire place was lookin' and not me.

I was just the big fat mama bear, it should be the happiest time of my life and his life, but once again it wasn't. I didn't feel that he was really up for this whole trip. He was out somewhere most of the time these days after work. One day that really sticks out in my memory is—on the way home from work we did our usual shopping bit at Cleveland after work and were having a beer or two on the boat going home. He leapt off at Karra Garra Island and said I'll see ya at work tomorrow. Oh great. I thought to myself. Here I was nearly 7 months pregnant and I could get all the shopping off the boat and then get it all on to the Macleay jetty, and then up and into the car and then I can unload it when I get home. Bloody Charming. Other than that the bastard sat opposite me at work and also just spent the past hour shopping with me and could have mentioned this at any point in time before now. He just didn't seem to care for me anymore.

Jarmas continued to come and go as he pleased and really, after Deric moved to the mainland he basically lived at Deric's. Deric was really a better catch than me anyway, because he had drugs in plentiful supply and I did not. I was only carrying his baby, big deal.

During Christmas Holidays I moved over to Deric's as well because it was a lot easier to get to work and I could get up later and be home earlier. Deric's girlfriend babysat Stuart at this time, while the rest of us went to work. Once the holidays were over I had to go back to Macleay, for Stuart to go to school. I felt I just may be going home alone at this time. Shortly after the hols, Deric quit work, because the other business he was in was taking up all his time. Then I quit because I was just getting too big and awkward to continue on. So naturally, Jarmas quit as well because there was no fun in it any more. No one to have cones with at lunch time, no one to race home in the afternoon, (a regular occurrence) and no reason for Jarmas to work if' no one else was. Too bad about the $8,000 worth of Transit Van we just went into debt for, in my name, and too fucking bad about the bills and the oncoming baby. Unbelievable!

Jarmas still continued to come and go as he pleased. I should have stopped him right then and there, but I did not. I was carrying his baby and he was the Daddy, so I must try at all costs to make this work. I didn't want to be a single mother with 2 different assorted kids, and furthermore I loved him. For what real reasons, I'm buggered if I know any more, but he was there in my heart and there to stay.

We fought a lot and yelled a lot and I kicked him out a lot, but he always came back sorry, and usually with flowers, and I always forgave him.

The day Ebony came was a doozey. I had asked numerous times if he could fix the water pump for me because without it there was no hot water. My back was killing me, carrying this extra load, and I wanted to be able to have a bleedin' shower. I know how unreasonable this may seem, but that's the type of guy I am. The chick down the road, who was almost as pregnant as me, was having similar problems with her bloke. He was s'posed to mow the lawn before going out to play! The pair of them just left on their motor-bikes and didn't give 2 shits about their respective, fat wives.

I decided Jarmas could go live with Steve (the bloke) and Sandy, decided, Steve could go live with Jarmas. Well, the 2 of us women decided to leave all their crap in the middle of the 2 houses in the end, which basically is a deserted, grassy street. **My street,** and nearly no one used it but me. Sandy and I then went back to my place, with a couple of largies each, to calm our nerves. The pair of idiots came back from their escapades just after dark, which is too late to do anything. I told Jarmas to fuck off and not to come back and also to forget all about his unborn child, who he doesn't give a shit about anyway. Sandy told Steve to f-off as well and they both left. They came back again a few hours later and were bashing about in the pump shed, obviously trying to fix something. How bloody stupid, trying to do a job in the dark that could have been done quite easily in the hours of light. Then they left again.

Sandy and I finished our beers and went to bed. A short time after that, my waters broke. Sandy was there to help me and to love me. Ha. Ha. When I tried the shower it had thankfully been fixed, so I stood under it for a long time with the hot running on my back, and tears running down my face and blood running down my legs. Sandy came in and asked me if I wanted her to go and get him. I thought for awhile about it all and then said, "Yes, go get him, I can't let him miss the birth of his first child, Our Child." When he did get back he was still half pissed and casually said, "I think I'll go have a nice hot shower." The smart bastard. I'm by this time in serious pain and all he wants is a shower and a cuppa. He still had no concern for me, and at no point did he ask if I was OK. The ambulance arrived at the back of the house and I had to walk through the long grass, and I mean long, with towels between my legs to get to it. (Stupid idiots came up the wrong track) At this point Mr Fucking Jarmas realised he had left his pot at Steve's place and dashed off to get it, saying I'll catch ya at the Jetty.

Why did I bother? Why did I ever bother? I felt alone. What's new? He did manage to make it to the jetty before the Special Boat came. Lucky for him. When we got to the mainland, he jumped in the front of the Ambulance, so if Ebony was born on the way there he would have missed out anyway. Two and a half hours from the waters breaking to **the birth of my beautiful little daughter, Ebony Jasmin.**

Another little baby child is born, and her mumma cried.

Jarmas was absolutely stoked, over the moon, wrapped, thrilled. **Look what HE had done. What a clever fellow.** He still never hugged me or even hardly looked at me. He just took off down the hallway chasing the doctor with **HIS Daughter,** who had bubbles in the belly. All I could do was lay back and be glad the hard part was over. I could hear him though, all the way down the corridor, "What are you doing to my baby, what are you doing to my Daughter." Then he spent the next hour on the blower, ringing all his relatives, to tell them HIS exciting news and that HE had a baby girl, Ebony Jasmin, and then he left. Thanks for coming. He was so proud of himself and he was so proud of his little princess. *A little Ray of Sunshine has come into the world. A little Ray of Sunshine in the shape of a girl.*

A few weeks later we had organized to go to Bendigo to visit all the rest of his family with the Little Princess as she came to be known. I was so looking forward to this holiday. The whole family, my little family was going on holiday. How wonderful, I really had a family now, I fitted in and further more we were off on holiday, all the way to Victoria. The following week, a mate of mine told me how much Deric was looking forward to this holiday too. Well, you couldn't expect the Bastard to leave his drug dealer behind, could you? I spat the dummy about this at first and said he could take his bloody mate with him and show him off to the Family, because I wasn't bloody coming. After a while I realised I would be cutting off my nose to spite my face, so I decided to go anyway.

I had a great time meeting all the relo's, and seeing all the sights of Bendigo. I had met his sisters before and his Mum and Dad just briefly on the Island when I was half way preggers. I seemed to fit in well with all of them. I still didn't feel completely at home though, but that was only because he didn't seem to care for me anymore. I'd only put on about 2 stone since meeting him, but after all that was partly his fault.

I really hoped that when Ebony Jaz was born, that things would change for the better and that Jarmas would become more of a family man. As usual, I was wrong. It was worse actually because he stayed away more often, like earlier, except now I hardly ever got to go with him because it would take too long to get the Baby ready. He might have missed a boat or something, or a big deal . . .

So he fucked off on a regular basis and I told him to fuck off on a regular basis and life went on anyway. Then it got a bit more serious because he hit me as well. This was nothing new to me, I've lived through violence before, but he was more violent than Daddy 1, much more. He was also about a foot taller and had lived in and out of jails since he was 12.

One night some friends saw him disappear along the beach front at Corroborrie Point with some sleaze bag from Lamb Island. When I got home from the same event, he was at home in my bed asleep. I woke him up and told him to get his arse out of my bed and go because I wouldn't put up with a liar and a cheat. He hit me backwards into the hallway and then he hit me again and again and when Kellie tried to stop him he hit her as well. We were both terrified and left my house and went up the road with the kids and stayed away for the night. The next day he was gone, which was often the case. It still always hurt me and I wished he was still here. This is bloody stupid I know, but I still loved him. **It was a love, hate relationship. We both loved to hate each other.**

After a few more weeks he'd come back again, or phone and say how sorry he was and 'please, please forgive me. I love you, Nicky, I always will'.

I always wanted to forgive him, sometimes it took a lot longer for me to forgive him, it just depended on how much he hurt me.

One weekend, the weekend of John Boy's 22nd I was actually invited over to a party at the place down the road from Jarmas' temporary home. John Boy was a good friend of mine too so I made the cake, as I would, A Bart Simpson Cake at that. We even put a joint in his mouth which was the only bit of the cake used. The rest of it ended up squashed in faces and as skating stuff on the polished floor. Great fun, but a waste of a good cake. At about 10pm Jarmas wanted to go home. He was here all week, and he partied all week. He was also stuffed for this reason and wanted me to go home with him now! I convinced him that he should go and take Ebony and Stu and I'd wander home later. "Come on Jarmas I've been stuck on that Alcatraz Island all week every week, with kids and others; give me a break for fuck's sake. He did.

About 2 hours later everyone decided to go to the Casino, my favorite place. I'm going. Six people were going and we could share the taxi money. Yes I'm going. By the time the taxi came half the people that were going had passed out and the other half weren't going without that half. So guess what? There was only me and Matt left. I looked out the door and here was the cab and Mat was in the back saying, "Are you gonna pike it too." No way. Then he said to me that he had no shoes to get in and that Jarmas' would fit him. So we took off in the cab and went up to Jarmas' place. I sneaked in quietly and asked him if Mat-Mat could borrow his shoes. He replied, "eerhhgggggggrrrrrrr!. That's a yes. I stuffed the $500.00 that he'd given me earlier inside his pillow case, grabbed the shoes and ran back to the cab.

Mat and I had a wonderful night we hitched most of the way to the casino as there was now only the two of us to pay the fare. After about three hours of gambling, which I was winning, I lost him. I looked everywhere for him but he'd apparently been thrown out for dancing on the roulette wheel. Fair enough. He had all my winnings though and I had now run out of money. Looks like I'm hitching home as well.

I did hitch home, but caught a cab from round the corner from Jarmas' place. As I went past his place he started up and followed me back to the party house from the night before. When we both pulled up there, he asked "Where the fuck have you been?" To which I replied, "None of your fucking business."

Run Nick.

I ran out the back of the house which was the stupidest thing I could have done, because the back verandah was about 40 feet off the ground. Jarmas caught me up here out the back and held me upside-down over the verandah. Saying the same words. Where the fuck have you been? No one stopped him and no one helped. After that for a few minutes, he just let me up and then bashed the shit out of me then he left, and with the kids.

I pulled myself together after awhile and caught yet another taxi then back to Jarmas, where he'd fortunately left the kids. Then I went to the Bay for another lonely boat home. This time I could hardly walk though and I was not going to forgive him. He also had no reason to bash me other than his own insecurity.

I did forgive him.

One time during one of our many separations, (if you could call it that) he asked if he could have Ebony for the night so I could go to the Dart competition on the Island. I was so stupid, I should have known he'd never have done anything just for me. He said he would send Ebony back in the morning with my sister. Huh! When I rang him in the morning he said, **"you're not getting Ebony back till you stop partying."** Admittedly I was partying a fair bit, but after nearly 2 years of waiting round for him, who wouldn't. Well I ended up ringing him up later and stirring him up as much as I possibly could. I had half a party going on in the background, so I just kept ringing and telling him I had a few blokes there with me and I was enjoying their company. I had fallen over earlier and told him on the phone that this bloke was patching up my knee for me. I knew I'd worked him up enough, and I knew why. Mr Jarmas would come racing over to the Island, any which way he could, ifin' he thought he was being robbed. I also knew he would not leave Ebony behind, because a nappied child, had just been touched up there at the house he was staying at, about a week before.

So being the alcoholic that I am, I got drunker and went to bed. I woke at about 4am. I went out to get a drink, a skull of milk or something for the dry horrors. Sue and Lyns were sitting at the table, still and Malinda said, "Oh you've got no idea what happened after you crashed out Nicky. Well that's bloody obvious—I've been asleep for a few hours. Then they tell me Mr J. had been standing outside the windows for a few hours and the bloke who wasn't really looking after my sore knee or me; had apparently followed me to bed, though he was uninvited and the door was shut. Mr J. saw this bloke come into my bedroom and as he took off his second boot, Jarmas was through the bedroom window and grabbed young Shane and dragged him out the room and out of the house to beat the shit out of him.

It was a bit cheeky of Shane anyway I guess, especially when the door is shut. Jarmas bashed him within an inch of his life and I know the only reason I didn't cop it this time is because he WAS watching. Lyns and Sue had to stop Jarmas from killing him and he dragged himself off through the bush to get away. I knew none of this of course, till now, and now I wanted to know which way he went. Jarmas I mean. He still had my Ebony. Someone reckoned he went up the Island towards the Hot Bread Kitchen, which means to me he could only have gone to one place. Firstly I went down the phone box and rang the police, mainly because I ripped the phone out of wall earlier and thrown it out the window. I told them that there was going to be a **murder on this Island tonight** if I don't get my Daughter back. The police told me that I was on tape and if there was a murder on Macleay tonight they know who did it. And I told them I didn't give a shit and hung up.

Then I went to the house where I knew Mr Jarmas would be, up the far end of the Island. I knew also that the bloke who lived there was away, which meant his lady friend was home alone, well home with Jarmas and my Daughter anyway. I knocked on the door loudly. I was so agro and shaking in my boots with rage, but I knew I was right. I knew he was here.

"Where my fucking Daughter, Sandy?" I know she's here.

"She's not here Nicky," was the flimsy reply. "She's not here, I'm the only one home."

"Bullshit, where is she."

Then I could see over her shoulder, a tall dark, shadowy figure that was obviously trying desperately to pull up a pair of jeans. I could also see a small curled up figure in the bed.

"I'm not completely stupid Jarmas," I yelled. And pushed past Sandy to get my Daughter.

Jarmas then came into the foreground via some other doorway and grabbed me by the throat.

"Just fuck off home Nicky. You're not getting her back. I'd rather see her go to a home than to see you get her."

I got away from him and got back in the van and locked all the doors. Then I yelled out to him, "I've already rung the police about you nearly killing Shane, and they're on there way, Bastard Breath." He always had one or two warrants, so I knew this would put the wind up his arse, and after all I devised this whole plan anyway. By this time it was nearly first boat time and I yelled out again, "Put my Daughter in her seat Jarmas, and you'll just have enough time to escape before they get here. Just put her in the car Now!" "I'll even drop you at the boat and you'll still be free.*" Red, Gold and Green, Freedom, Love, and Peace. HUH!* Finally he got Ebony and strapped her in her car seat, and then he got in the back along side of his Little Ray of Sunshine. We drove in silence to the main jetty, where only a few short months earlier, we'd gone for Ebby's birth. He got out and stalked up the jetty and I yelled at him again, **"Just remember, Mr. Fucking Norton, I gave you you're freedom."**

"Get fucked," was all he could manage.

When I got back home, I told the girls what went down and that he was gone. It took them about half the day but they finally convinced me I should leave and do it Now. I wanted to see Shane first, so I went round to his place to see how he was. Oh my God! Oh my God! I've never seen anything so horrific in my whole life before. I held him and just cried. I didn't know what to say. All I could do was look at his face and cry. He was almost unrecognizable. He had an obviously broken cheekbone, and his left eye was resting on that. All the blood had been washed off, but he looked purple all over. I was lying on the lounge floor next to him, he was in serious pain and this was all my fault. I felt so terrible for him and there was nothing I could do about it. I wanted my daughter back and I got her. The rest of his family was there too and giving me filthy looks, but after all I did not actually punch him myself and I also did not invite him in to my bed.

The rest of Shane's family wanted to start some sort of war with Jarmas and whoever wanted to join in. I felt this was like taking on the Mafia at the time and I told Shane he was probably best off to do as I was and to get the fuck out of here. The family were still ranting and raving as I left, about different ways to kill the bastard. I told Shane once more to leave well enough alone. Goodbye Shane, I'll see you again somewhere, someday.

Right then, the decision's made. Now all I had to do was put it into action. Firstly I took the Transit Van round to Billy's place and had him do a check on it all and fix the bonnet which didn't open, and managed to get him to throw in a spare. Next I got young Stuart to work scrubbing out the wheelie bins. One was mine, and one that I knocked off on the way back from Shane's. Then pack. Shit, what am I packing. This was my home for nearly 7 years. Too bad Nix, **don't think about it, just pack, and hurry the fuck up.**

What do we need—everything, including this house. No, just get everything for setting up a flat, and some books, toys, kids' clothes, and all the photos, just in case I don't get back for a while.

All the pots and pans, tupperware, cutlery and kitchen shit went into one wheelie bin while it was already situated in the back of the van. Then a few bags of personal shit, mops and brooms, 2 eskies, micro, turned off the fridge and freezer, locked all the windows and doors and off we went. We only had a couple of hours to get the barge and get off this Island,(Alcatraz) and like Lyns Bag said, he'll probably come back after dark and have another go. Not necessarily at me but to get his daughter. Which apparently is all he ever gave a fuck about to start with. Bloody beautiful isn't it. Us women just end up being the **receptacle** for some of these so called men.

As you can imagine I was pretty spun out and stressed out and sort of depressed, but I guess what must have kept me going was fear. I really couldn't believe what J. had done to Shane's face, I also couldn't believe that it was the bloke I'd been in love with for so long who had done this. After the first scary scene of getting off the barge and up through Capalaba and the next few suburbs, and finally getting over the Gateway, I felt safe.

The kids had Macdonalds (which we've since changed to The Golden Arches, for secretive reasons) and they had both passed out with *the rocking rollin' ridin'* of the engine.

When I got to Eumundi I thought I deserved an Ouzo or two for the rest of my trip, isn't it a pity they sell them 3 for 10 bucks, so that's the best deal. Grab a bargain I always say. I opened the first can about 5 minutes out of town (maybe 2) and then lit an accompanying joint. Ahh bliss. Well I say this must be the end of Chappie 10.

YOU THINK!!!

Read on!

Well naturally I was getting more crazy by the minute. I only smoked about half of the joint but I continued to drive on and watch the white lines and breaks go by. It's definitely starting a new life or turning over a new leaf so to speak. Actually I started to feel sort of happy about the whole thing. Sort of.

A new path. Something had to change anyway, I was getting nowhere fast *"Ain't it just a crying shame, you've only got yourself to blame,"* was playing on the radio, just to amuse me, no doubt. By the time I got through Gympie I opened the second can of Ouzo all alone and I smoked the other half of the joint and the little children slept on. It's all just an adventure to them I figure and if the Mummy is happy the little children will be happy as well. It follows. I bloody well think so anyway and one must sometimes convince themselves of these things just to make it through. **OK? OK!**

We were heading for Hervey Bay anyway, so I had one last one just out of Maryborough for the last hurdle. I think we got to my mate Sandy's place about 9pm and it was pissing down rain. I was so glad to finally get there. Sandy and I sat up for awhile chatting and I told her all the latest that had been happening in my unhappy life. None of it was what I had hoped and planned for. None of it.

Sandy had one son Ryan who use to go to school with Stuart on Macleay a year before, so they were both happy about the present set-up. Stuart shared Ryan's room and Ebony and I were in the spare room, which she fortunately had. Sandy didn't mind the situation either, it helped her out a bit financially, and it was only for a few weeks till I found a house or flat to rent in the area. Hervey Bay is a really nice spot, better in many ways than the Island and you didn't have to catch a boat. I couldn't get Stuart in to school until I knew where I would be living though, so really I couldn't mess about.

I found a two bedroom flat the next week with the help of another old friend of mine, Kellie. She was, in actual fact, living in Hervey Bay as well, and her Mum was working for P.D.R. Reality. How fortunate for me. The place was called "Ocean Breezes", but don't let that conjure up any shore front palace, it was a complete dump and I hated it, we had to live somewhere though and this looked like it. I just wished I could snap out of this depression.

My life was so messy at this point and there wasn't much I could do about it. I joined the library, for something to do. I got out a few books on alcoholism, obsessive behaviour, drug addicts and all that exciting stuff. According to them once an alcoholic always an alcoholic, and once a junkie always a junkie. Great, well for me it reckoned, one day at a time because the whole picture of never having another drink, was just much too depressing. It's just too hard to get your mind round it, like not going to any parties, or barbies, or pubs, or clubs, no large groups, no small groups—the casino and race track would have to be off the agenda; the list goes on. I could go on. I won't though because to this day I drink, though at this particular point in time I had actually been off the piss for nearly a month. It is hard for non-alcoholics to understand all this, but it's basically just a chemical imbalance. After just a few drinks there's no turning back. There's varying degrees of alcoholism of course, but for the most of us it's just a case of **drink till there's none left or till you fall over, whichever comes first.**

At the same time as this I also got out a book called "Unconditional Love", and read that. It's obvious that I feel it's all my fault *and I could have been better,* should have been nicer and less drunk and obnoxious, but thinking back now I don't, because I really DID do all the right things for the first two years and nothing was going to change this man and his Gypsy ways. I can understand all of it more now but after all I am ten years older and wiser.

I got Stuart in to Kawangan School, the 2nd school of his short years. He didn't seem bothered about any of it really and he made friends easily. He had friends over the back of the flats already and he had Ryan to play with on the weekends. Kellie lived up the other end of Hervey Bay and her son Ricky was one of Stuart's lifelong mates, so he was happy all round.

Ebony was different though, she played up a lot more than usual and she started shitting on the floor on a regular basis. It was obvious she missed her father and also her friend Stephanie, who I'd been babysitting for about a year and a half. She'll get used to the change I thought, she'll pull up and get used to our new life. Time went on.

Jarmas finally found me. He got some woman to ring Sandy's and ask for me, and when I got to the phone he said, "Ehhh! I found you." We talked a bit and he wanted to come up and see Ebony, and he wanted us to talk more. He wanted to know where we were. Where he stood now. Oh no! I couldn't deny that I still loved him, I always probably will. I organized to meet him somewhere in the Bay. So in a few days he arrived. He'd rented a room for the night and bought some Chinese for dinner and we all went back to the room like a happy little family, so it would seem to the onlooker any way.

We talked a lot about what had happened and why. He blamed the piss and I blamed the drugs and his wheelin' and dealin' gypsy lifestyle. I never knew where he was from one day to the next. Anyhow he wanted to make another go of it and naturally so did I. He was going to come up as often as he could and see how things went for the next few months. Oh how excellent! I was happy again. I hadn't failed completely, not yet. I had my wonderful darling Jarmas back and we would work it out. We should work it out, after all we had a beautiful daughter to stay together for and this was my 2nd go at this relationship\mother bit. The main reason of course is always love and there was no doubt about that!

He came up the following week and then the week after that, but because he had to hitch-hike up there he then started to come up only once a fortnight. After awhile he asked if he could get the Transit Van back so he could come up more often. I naturally agreed because I wanted to see him more often, but I wasn't ready to go back. The next week was Ebony's 2nd Birthday and he would be back up for that and it would be much easier to bring all her presents and stuff too.

On the 29th of May nineteen ninety-two the Little Ray of Sunshine turned 2 years old. Her wonderful, wonderful Father turned up with two old mates and they all went to the pub. I wanted to be with Jarmas so me and Sandy and Kellie and all the kids went too. I started drinking after a while, well everyone else was, so what the hell. **I finally drank again after nearly three months.** I was wonderfully slim too and looking real good in a pair of jeans no less. A few hours and quite a few jugs later we all went back to the flat and partied on. Jarmas told me he was going later on, so I conned one of his mates Steve into staying the night. One of his mates was Mat from the Island, the one I got bashed over, and for nothing. The next day they all left and it was the last time I ever was to lay eyes on the Father of my 2nd child for nearly three years.

I went through some serious pain then. I'd rung the place where he was staying and Ian, another old mate from Macleay Island, told me, "He's gone Nicky. He left with all his shit."

"Is he on his way up here already, Ian?"

"No Nicky, he's gone to Victoria, back to Bendigo."

I nearly dropped the phone. I was completely dumbfounded at what I'd just heard. I could not believe it. I had been conned again and now I was alone once more, now with two kids and car-less as well. I really went to pieces then but still I had no money to do anything much about it.

Thanks for coming!

CHAPPIE 10

MR. CASUAL

After another depressing month, now without a car, Mat turned up one day and wanted to stay a night or two because he had stuff to attend to in Maryborough and Hervey Bay. I didn't mind at all and I could certainly do with some adult company. He stayed for awhile and then went out for the day. Later that night he arrived back with his ruck-sack. I asked him about what had happened after they all left here on that dreaded Birthday night. He filled me in a bit more about what Jarmas did and how he had planned the whole thing. He had planned all along to take off with the Van and that's all he was interested in, in the end. He would have taken his daughter, The Little Ray of Sunshine, but he had already tried that, so I guess he thought the Van would have to suffice.

Matt and his other mate had left here and gone all the way to Victoria with my darling Jarmas and also he'd gone straight to some chicky-babe's place, some chicky-babe that he'd obviously been in touch with in the past few months. Well that was enough reason for me and off we went to the nearest pub, Matt, Ebony, Stuart and this old, depressed version of the former Nicky. It's not good to drink excessively when you're really depressed about something or someone.

We stayed for a couple at the pub and then went back to my daggy old flat with a bottle or flagon of Port, I think it was. After which I spent the rest of the night spewing on the toilet floor. You'd think that would be enough to stop anyone from drinking. I made an arse of myself and was still curled up on the toilet floor in the morning and so no one could go to the loo if they tried. The next night we had drinks again and I ended up cuddled up on the lounge with Mat. Whoops!

Matt didn't seem to mind about this occurrence at all and we spent the next day mostly in bed. Mat-Mat came back on a regular basis after that for the next few weeks. We had a great time together, most of it drunk. He was great with the kids though and took them out on long bike rides down the esplanade, while I slept in occasionally. We went swimming a lot and fishing sometimes and life was generally good. I still had my finances to clear up though, and I'd have to start thinking about going back to my own place or at least to stop paying dead rent. I was paying my house off, paying $90.00 a week rent and paying $240.00 a month for a **fucking Transit Van** that I no longer possessed. I did finally have someone in my house renting it though so that helped a little, but it also meant I couldn't go back there, not right now anyway.

Ian Grimm, the bloke who Jarmas had been living with at Kingston, offered me a room in his house free of charge. All I would have to do is cook and clean for him and his flat mate Mick. This was really excellent for me at the moment and would sort out all my money troubles. I had no more reasons to be living so far from home any more. Jarmas was obviously not coming back, to bash me or otherwise.

Grimm came up with a big trailer and I moved us all back to Brisbane. Mat and John Boy were both there that day too so I had plenty of helpers and not much to move. So back to Brissy and off to yet another school with young Stuart. I would have gone straight to the Island but I could not and this wasn't so bad. I had no rent and no house payments either. All I had left still was the van payments. That

76

bloody van. That bastard Man. Still driving around in my vehicle with his latest **slut.**

I was broken hearted by the whole deal with Jarmas and was always looking for clues as to where he actually went. Well on this particular day Ian's latest phone bill came in and there; all over the bill, were dozens of calls made to a place called Wedderburn, which is a suburb in Victoria. U-Huh! I'm sure and positive if that bastard can find me I can bloody well find him too. So I rang the regularly occurring phone number, (Ian was in the background, saying tell him he owes me 50 bucks for the phone) and I said exactly the same word to Jarmas as he had used a few months before. **"Huh, I found ya."**

"How the fuck did you get this number," were his first words. One would expect him to ask after his Little Ray of Sunshine (what a joke). Well the phone call went extremely badly and he did not want to know me or his daughter and when I moaned about the car and my finances and the fact he was driving the car I was paying for. He replied, "Do you want me to get my violin out, bitch?."

"You don't play the fucking violin, you play the mouth organ you fucking bla bla."

Then crunch, down smashed the phone with a couple of extra crashes as if the receiver was actually his head. Ian frowned upon this of course but I still spent the next half hour swearing my head off about Jarmas Fucking Norton and how he had purposefully used and abused me and then taken what he wanted after the fact. I really should have considered myself lucky that he didn't have my Ebony, and that he'd only scarpered with the car. Naturally I did not. I could only get agro about all that he'd done to me and how many years were wasted on a **lying, cheating, criminal, bastard like him.** All this tied together, was a bloody good excuse to drink and to get drunk.

I did drink a hell of a lot during this session of my life. I mean a hell of a lot. Sometimes I think back about it and wonder how we survived at all. I wonder how Ian's house got cleaned or how any dinner ever got made or even how young Stuart got to school each day. It did all get done though, I just don't know how.

It was during this binge drinking session that I crossed the line and slept with my house mate Ian. (shock horror) Now Ian had always fancied me since we were about 11. We basically grew up together on the Island. Ian did also know that Mat and I were having a casual affair and we even called each other "CAS". Men are men though, and as Mat was not about on a regular basis and I was extremely drunk, Grimm thought it was about time he got his share of the goods.

I really think Ian wanted the whole picture with me but taking advantage of a drunken idiot is not the way for love to blossom. I didn't want any sort of relationship anyway, after all, I'd just been through the relationship from hell. This was precisely why Mat fitted in because he was "CAS" and didn't care what I was doing or why and vicky-verky. I was disgusted in myself and I was pissed off with Grimm more, because we'd been friends for so long now and once this shameful act had happened he just kept harrassing me. Mat still came over once a week or whenever the fit hit and Grimm said nothing. Each time after Mat was gone the filthy little creation said, "come on Nick it's my turn now, stop holding out on me. This is my house you're living in you know, don't play your silly little games with me."

I was horrified. I so much wished it had never happened, but it was too late for wishes. All I wanted to do was get out of there, and fast. I rang me best mate Pam and asked for help. "Can you possibly get a trailer, A.S.A.P. and help me get myself out of here and back home. The only real home I've ever had."

"No worries Nick," said Pam. "We can organize all of that, hopefully for the weekend. I can borrow a trailer from Carol, and Ray gets off at lunch time on Saturday so we'll be able to get the afternoon barge." Excellent! Me and my mate Pam could (and still can) always organize a mission of this caliber.

Well as it turned out, Friday afternoon I was sitting in Pam's lounge when Ray entered the scene and then the two of them disappeared together. After a time sitting there alone I heard yelling and swearing from both parties. This was really nothing unusual to me, but they kept getting louder and louder. By this time I was on the phone to Sue telling her what I was planning. Suddenly Ray appeared from beyond still yelling and Pam's in tears. Sue said "Is that Jarmas? I'm coming straight over to get you. What's going on?"

At this point I realised they were fighting about the plans for the weekend, and how dare Pam put him up to helping out, or designate little jobs for him when he works all week. Apparently he was sick and tired of her helping everyone out and being used all the time. "Used for Suckers, all the time, fucking idiot, blah, blah blah, ra ra ra".

I finished the call with Sue quick smart and she was coming to get me. I was bloody glad too, because honestly, the yelling and screaming really gets to me and I was already a nervous wreck.

I ended up in tears as well and Pam got up Ray a little bit more then. Oh shit!

Sue arrived, thank Christ and I could leave. Not before thanking Pam very much and explaining to Ray that I intended paying all costs and also shouting them at the Bowls Club for lunch and drinks. The only reason I couldn't do it myself is because **Fucking Jarmas Fucking Norton stole my car. OK!"** On that note I left.

Well the car was the only problem so, buy a car Nicky, and stop fucking about. Sue and I spent that evening marking all the cars under $300.00 in the paper. Saturday morning off we went to Brisbane's Cheapest Cars, which is slap bang in the middle of the Valley. There were a few real cheapies but the best was a blue Datsun 180 B which was pretty straight, almost passable tyres and hardly any rust. The radio and lighter worked as well so that was a bonus

. What wasn't a bonus at all, was the Car Yard Bloke took the plates off. Oh, bummer, I never knew that they had to do that. Oh well it was bought and paid for and that's that. I decided to follow Sue and to stay right up her arse, so the oncoming traffic could not see that there were no plates. I was willing to take the risk if it was going to get me out of Grimm and back to my place. We had to go over the Story Bridge and there just happened to be about 10 cops on the bridge-that morning. They were walking along discussing some shit and fortunately for me they turned around and went the other way just at the right moment. What naughty girls we were. Well me anyway. Sue followed me right back to Grimm' place and then she had to get going. I went in and got all my personal stuff together and shoved as much as I could into my new $200.00 unregistered car. Then Stuart and Ebony and I got the same barge I intended to get anyway and we were going home. The woman that was renting my place had suddenly moved out a few days previous.

It was another painful time in some ways—all the old memories came flooding back. The one I loved and was going to spend the rest of my life with was gone and here was I, back in my little house on Macleay without him. Getting drunk with heaps of old mates will solve any little depressions. For a short time anyway. I realised Jarmas had been back here and helped himself to whatever he thought was rightfully his. Anything that was decent or worth anything was gone. Who was really to know what he had taken and what the bitch that was renting had taken. Whatever was gone was gone. No use crying over spilt milk. (or beer)

I did settle down a bit here for a while, got back into Island style living. Got Stuart back into his old school with his old teacher. Ebony had her mate Stefie back and everyone was happy. Nearly everyone. Then Mat came back. From where? Who knows, up north somewhere probably. That just finished off the happy family picture though. It was great. He was great. He helped me to forget. He made me feel young and sexy. The kids loved him too. He just fitted in so perfectly with everything, Plus my Mum and Dad thought he was great as well. I was just so happy, so deliriously happy.

Something had to come along and stuff it up, didn't it? AND of course it did. It's not that I'm pessimistic it just always seems to happen. This time it was in the form of warrants for Matt, who got seriously drunk and decided to do the time and get it over with. So he was taken away from me and just when I thought it was RIGHT. I missed him terribly, it was a new pain in my heart and I wanted him, bodily

I mean, I don't think I ever really felt like that before. I think I even wrote a few sick letters to him one night when I was pissed and lonely. It was really bad because I knew he still loved and wanted me too but we just couldn't be together now.

The time (his time) seemed to drag on forever. I did go and visit him one day with his Dad. His father picked me up off the main jetty in his own boat and over to the mainland we went. I felt like a big jerk because I'd never met the man before and here I was going to the jail house to visit his son. When we got to the mainland, I got a few bits and pieces at the shop for Mat, some bike mags and stuff, and then off to the jail. This also was a new experience for me and I was surprised at myself for even going. I had always said to Jarmas that if he ended up in jail I'd never visit him and that I'd never take kids to the jail either. Here was I doing just that for some other bloke. When we got there and Mat finally came from his confined area, he just looked so terrified, he looked like a big baby boy, who was sorry for being so naughty. His father and he chatted a bit and I gave him his few little pressies. None of this was much fun and I couldn't wait to get out of the place and back home. Finally when his Father and I hit the boat this time he pulled out a six pack and handed me one, I relaxed a lot more then and we had a much better chat on the trip home. It's amazing how **XXXX** can relax you.

When Mat did get out it was one day earlier than we thought, and the greatest surprise! I was in bikinis and almost upside down cleaning out all the cockys after the Pest Control bloke had been, when someone wolf whistled from outside in the darkness. I had no idea it was him and ran to cover up my lumpy white body and in he strolled with a huge bunch of flowers and a shaved head. Probably a carton too, no doubt.

We cruised along happily again for awhile but both of us liked a drink or three, but only one of us was the jealous type and that was him. Uh Oh! Here we go again. He was always late home; meaning he was never back when he said he would be. He always had his mates with him and he was nearly always drunk when he had his mates with him. Don't get me wrong here I love mates and drunken rowdy parties, just not every day and not always at my bloody place. He just wasn't there for me any more—he was there for his own selfish reasons, himself, alone.

The crunch came one afternoon when he was late as usual, and he brought a mate. We had been invited to a barbie at my Boss' house (the bloke I cleaned for) and I wanted to be on time, which was 5.00pm. Shorty, the boss, was a ex-army person and you know what they're like about punctuality. I do of course, because of Dad and his ways, five minutes late and it's all over. Anyway, being the wonderful person I am, I was ready with potato salad and coleslaw, my A1 rissoles and half a carton for the night, and all of us looking immaculate. Naturally my next move was to leave the half pissed Mat and his idiot, loser mate behind, so I would be on time. This was my first wrong move. I did tell him his shirt was ironed and if he wanted to come up—I'd see him later. NOT good enough, Nick.

Mat obviously sat at home with his mate and got way drunker. Then he got pissed off about me not being there. Then he got Jealous. Then he came to Shorty's. There was only a few people left at Shorty's and by the time Mat got there most had gone, leaving my Sister and me and Shorty of course. The first thing he did was tip his stubby into my cigarettes, purposely. I was not impressed and probably swore at him, which is natural under the circumstances. I think he sat there for about five minutes and then he went for Shorty, and then me, and finally my sister copped it as well for trying to save me. He just went completely wild, like nothing I've ever seen before. He grabbed anything he could and smashed it, he kicked and punched and wiped out tables of food, he just literally went berserk. Shorty had left somehow with a broken ankle and it was just Lyns and me and our kids left to witness the crazed animal in action.

Last of all when he seemed to have calmed down, he looked over at me sitting in a quivering heap on the chair and threw full stubbie across the room which hit me right on the knee-cap with an awful ka-thunk, and then he left. The pain was excruciating. Ahhhhhh!

After a short time Shorty arrived back with the ambulance people, who checked us out. I thought my knee was broken. The ambulance officer, Dad's mate, insisted he take me to the Doctor's to have it properly checked out. Malinda was OK, she did get thrown across the room but she was OK, just badly shaken and horrified that her daughter had to witness this shit. Turned out the knee was not broken, just very badly bruised and swollen, but poor ol' Shorty's ankle WAS broken and so was most of his house.

Lyns was so agro about the whole thing, you can't blame her for that, and I was just depressed. I had really hoped my Mat-Mat and I could make it. My fault as usual. I should've waited for him to shower and change and get rid of his mate. I should've waited for my man instead of running up to Shorty's to party. I should've obviously done anything but what I did do, BUT Should-ofs and Could-ofs are always too late. I s'pose I just didn't want to be fucked around with like the last time, with Jamas. I will do whatever I like, as he did and I'll do it when I like. So there! Mat was not Jamas though and should not have been treated the same. Maybe?

Well I guess that'll be the end of that, one would definitely think so, wouldn't one. **Fuck men anyway they're a complete waste of time and I've wasted E—FUCKING—NUFF!**

CHAPPIE 11

NICKY'S LITTLE INTERLUDE

It must be time to split this Popsicle Stand anyway. It's all bad news. It seems only the early days when I was a kid was this Island any good or any fun. Things change though—maybe for the better—maybe not. We all have to think at these sad points in our lives or at these really bad times, that things can and will get better. Of course we could also think that everything is as low as it goes, why bother going on. We have ta' go on to find out all the answers to why it didn't work out and again I'll have to say we learn by our mistakes. Well hopefully. I'm still learning by mine and hopefully my dull and boring story will help someone somewhere to learn by some of mine. Maybe my beautiful daughter, Ebony, will find what she is looking for and make no mistakes on the wayside.

More time went by, with me doing nothing but drink and party. Nothing at all, after washing and hanging, washing up, vacuuming, getting Stu off to school, the odd bit of mowing and raking, the occasional starter motor repair job and a spot of repainting. Then one day when the place just happened to look like a bomb hit it, the Real

Estate Lady phoned up and gave me one hour to clean up because she was bringing some possible buyers round to inspect the place. Shit, shit, shit.

The next hour I rushed around like a maniac, like the lady on the spray and wipe add, and cleaned the place up as best I could. When the prospective buyers arrived they had a quick look through the house and round the yard and didn't seem to me that they were too impressed. Next minute some blonde chick turned up to view the block next door and she came over to me, to ask about the large and swampy hole at the edge of the block, which was seemingly coming from my property. I dragged her aside and told her quickly and quietly that it was my grey water outlet and was to be fixed any day now and not to worry. I had to get rid of her quick smart or she could jeopardize the sale of my place. The Real Estate lady and the other people didn't stay very long though and I didn't think anything would come of it. Two days later I had a contract on the place and I had six weeks to pack up my life on Macleay and move on.

It was a good time and a bad time for me. It was, after all, what I had wanted but at the same time I sorta' didn't want to leave my Home. Change is often hard to cope with, especially when you're on your own and to make these life altering decisions is not as easy as it seems. I often wish I did have a man to make the lifetime decisions but then I wouldn't probably let anyone else decide for me anyway. Ha Ha.

It was all happening too fast for me, but it keeps the mind and body alive.

First, I looked at a couple of buses about the place, with big plans in mind of travelling round Australia, picking fruit and putting Stuart through Correspondence School. After a time I decided it was all too hard. What with the special license and all the expense of the whole issue even if you get a fairly cheap bus. I ditched that plan, mainly because a car (nissan Bluebird SSS with red and blue stripes, EX-BATHURST model) and an 18ft caravan came up for $3000. What would you do? So I thought this to be a bloody good purchase. It gave us a decent car and something to live in while working out the next step.

Jarmas entered my silly brain quite a lot at this time, and I even thought I'd drive down to Victoria and find him and tell him to "get in, it's your last chance," while wearing size 10 sexy, silk teddy. How sweet. I still loved him and wished things were different, but I ditched that idea too and I never ever wore that outfit. $84.00 it cost me too.

As it turned out, I had been conned because the car I bought would not actually tow the matching caravan. It just sunk down so low at the arse end, the whole wheel arches were almost touching and when I towed it up the Island it ended up with a big blow out in the back tyre. It was still a good deal but I would have ta' to get another 6 cylinder car to tow with.

I had a garage sale for a couple of weeks in a row and got rid of a lot of junk that you collect over the years, and I had been here for a few. On the last weekend, I took a trailer load of shit and sat at the Main Jetty with a "Steptoe and Son" type get-up and sold a few more bits and pieces. I also left most of the house furnished, because I had to fit our whole lives into that caravan. **Not too tricky for ya Nicky?**

Finally the day came to go. I had someone else to tow my caravan down to the barge and someone else again to collect my caravan from the other side. I was going to good ol' Pam's' temporarily, till I found a property of some description, hopefully with a livable premises on it. I didn't have a lot of money, only $18,000 to be exact and I knew that wouldn't go far when it comes to Real Estate. I knew I wanted a few acres, at least 5-20 with something on it even if it was just a weekender or an old farm house.

Pam and I checked every paper for houses and acreage in country areas. I went out with quite a few agents who kept showing me shit that I didn't want to see. They knew that, that was just the shit they wanted to sell. Possibly Washington Developments. They're all the same. You tell them exactly what you want, exactly what you're looking for and they show you one acre blocks, with little old ladies in curlers, either side, peering out the windows as we pull up. NO THANKS!

I finally get a decent sort of bloke, who showed me what I wanted to see and firstly maps of the whereabouts, the block description and all this in the comfort of Pam's own home. I did actually pick my next property while sitting in Pam's lounge. It had a nice cul-de-sac aspect and was also on a hill, had undulating slopes and was not flat and boring as all the blocks I'd seen so far. I was going to see the property in a few days and I was really excited about it. I'd been at Pam's nearly three months by now, a lot had happened and it was time to thank her immensely and get my act together again. Get my children settled again.

In between all this I was trying to teach Stuart Grade three, correspondence school, which wasn't going terribly well. He was supposed to sit in the Van for a few hours a day and do his school work, AND that's none too easy, plus I was definitely not cut out to be a Teacher.

I'd also had the pleasure of meeting Jim, Pammy's big brother. He was great fun and the greatest drunk as well. We went out to the Glen Hotel (of all places) and had a big night on the horses. Now Jim was a big gambler, well as far as I was concerned, and he put $50 on a "Sure Thing" and I put two bucks on "I Like Beer" If only I'd known at the time how much I like beer. It came up and I won about 50 bucks and Jim was spewing about it all because he'd lost $50. I was well pleased with myself. We got on excellently well together, he was such a character. Just one of the people who keeps you laughing all the time. A sharp dressed man too, slicked back long hair in a pony, possibly black silk trousers and a dress shirt to go with and winkle pickers (shoes) and to finish off some loud and leary tie! And he could dance as well. That's interesting in an Australian Bloke, but he was quite a bit older than me. I guess he was of the old school, where they were apparently still taught to be gentlemen.

The night before I went to view the property, all of us went to a party at Grimm' place. Pam, Ray, Jim and me. I ended up pretty pissy and Ray, Pam and Jim went home with the kids, and my kids as well. I decided, in my drunken stupor that I wanted to go and see Mat. He had been ringing me a bit too, so once I knew where he was staying I thought I could manage it from here. There was no one here to stop me so why not. Well I got as far as the bottom of the street, which is one of the biggest and most notorious hills in Bris. If not it should be. In those days too, there was no steel barrier at the bottom of the road and it was about there that I left the Bitumen. Actually there was nothing at the end either, so I actually went flying through the air and bottomed out on a grassy embankment.

After collecting my senses, I realised I was alive and everything seemed OK. I tried to start the car and it jumped into life. I kept having to wipe my eyes though. I didn't know what this shit was getting in my eyes all the time. A couple of seconds later I was reefed out of the car by someone and they turned off the car, grabbed the keys, locked up the car and carted me out of the gully.

I must've been still a bit shaken, but I finally noticed they were just Christian Living People, helping me out; and not Mr. Plodd. (Police) Well thank Christ for small miracles. They asked me where I came from and I told them—"Up the top of the hill." They took me back to Grimm' place, but they really wanted to take me to the hospital. Two of the ladies at the party tied a flannelette shirt round my head. They continued to party. I passed out shortly after that . . .

Morning came and I rang me ol' mate Pam and she told me I was a stupid bitch, and should be bitch slapped. She also told me to get my arse over there and she'd take me to her Doctor for stitches. I did all of the above and ended up with 32 stitches to the head. All of this was achieved before 11am when Mr. Real Estate agent was to arrive.

Pam kept saying "You can't go Naughty Nickers. You can't go like that. You've probably got concussion."

To which I replied, "I will be going, I've waited long enough to check this block out. I feel great as well, not even a headache. While I was in the bathroom, re-doing my ever-so-trendy scarf, Pammy whipped downstairs to greet the Real Estate bloke and told him the whole story. Shit Pam.

"I'm still going Pam, I'm, Fine!" Mr Real Estate was a bit nervous after this, thinking I'd pass out any minute, but that was not the case.

All the way to Nanango he told me about the block—the area—how it was booming, how to go about the finances and what to do about a house or a possible removal house. He was pretty informative and chatty really. When we finally got to Nanango he went round all the new estates and told me of prices for a house block. Then he drove to Kingaroy and showed me more new estates and told me more prices and after that he drove like the clappers out to The Block, which took about 10 mins. This makes the property 10 minutes to town; if you break the sound barrier anyway.

I didn't really fall for all his sales man bullshit. I just wanted to buy something and get settled again. The block was nice, the area seemed nice, only one other house in the whole street.

"I'll take it. Where's the dotted line?"

Mr. Real Estate asked me if I wanted to dig a shovel or two of dirt. Silly Bastard. Nope.

"Not worried about the dirt, let's go."

So off we went back through Nanango on our way to Brisbane. No Naughty Nickers. The bloke wants his money and there's no ANZ in Nanango Town only in Kingaroy. Oh dear. We have to back track through to Kingaroy to get the dollars. I told him not to worry, I'd get it tomorrow, but it would not be a sale today if ya don't get the money till tomorrow.

We got back to Pam about 6pm and he had his sale, and I had eight acres in Nanango. Finally I had found new hope and a new future for me.

Mat turned up again around this time, mainly to visit Pam and Ray of course, nothing to do with me or the fact that I had $18,000 in my pocket. He had court in a week over the rampage at Shorty's place. He wanted me to feel sorry for him and I did NOT. He wanted me to hold his hand in court and say I've forgiven him and ultimately he wanted me to forgive him and have another go.

In one way I really wanted someone to share my joy and to help me as I wasn't sure what I was in for. On the other hand, I wanted to say "look I did this all by myself". I wanted, as usual, to say, "It's all mine, I don't need a fucking man to put a roof over our heads, or to fix up everything in my life. They are only good for one thing and usually they're no good at that either." I was unsure.

Pam and I went to Drake House Removals to check out all the possibilities for my new home. I had the most wonderful day that day. I think Pam did too. When we first got to the place, the fella gave us a ladder and said "go for your life, ladies." We looked at each other like a pair of idiots and then twigged to what the caper was. We climb the ladder to look in each house. DUH!

So off we went with our ladder round the yard. It was great, there were heaps of old Queenslanders to choose from, some with all that fancy wrought iron lace work, some with wrap around verandahs, some with servant quarters. I quite fancy that idea. They all had great high ceilings and a lot with the fancy fret work between each room, fireplaces, and some with a wood stove in them. Then of course there were the much smaller ones, made of fibro or weather board without high ceiling, fireplaces, lace work and no verandah at all. These were the ones in my price range. The salesman (oh God not another salesman) was very helpful though. He told me how easy it was to add a bullnose or a verandah, or a bullnose verandah. He told me how to change 2 rooms into 3 and how to bring an outside bathroom in, in a couple of easy steps. He also showed me heaps of before and after pictures of what other people have done and how bleedin' clever they are.

The house I particularly wanted was 32,000 grand and the one I could afford with a small loan and some of my cash up front was $18,000. So I left with half a decision in my head.

Mat came back.

God he was gorgeous and so young. Maybe he can change; maybe he does love me and the kids. He still is great with the kids, he still is great in every way really, just not pissed. I wonder if anyone has ever thought that of me. NAH! We stayed together that night, and the next day I brought him up to look at the block. He was very mature for his age too, young Mat. The only problem ever was his jealousy. Really what it is, is that he thought I'd go for someone else as soon as I spoke to them, which of course was not the case at all. I'm just me and I like to talk to all the fellas. You learn a lot more than talking to silly women. I think I've always been the same. I'm still the same.

Mat was helpful. He told me a few things about where to put the house—from a backhoe operator's point of view. There was quite a big shelf of rock across the top section of the property and it would cost me a lot more for plumbing if I put the house up the front. If you buy acreage of any size at all you wouldn't want your house on the road edge anyway. We christened the block (if you know what I mean) and we left after that and checked out a few pubs in Kingaroy briefly and then went back to Pam's for a real drink.

The night before Mat went to court I got pissy and decided to go out. I was very confused at this point. His mate John boy thought I was a complete bitch and I should **Stand By My Man,** but he was going to court for losing the plot and bashing Shorty, my sister and me, though I did not press charges. It's a bit of a dilemma to stand by your man when he's going away for being a women basher and a violent drunk and crazy.

Court morning arrived, Mat still wanted me to come with him and Pam made it easier on me by saying "Just come with me Nick and we'll go shopping." Pam was elected to drive Mat and John Boy to the City. When we got to town I just sat in the car crying. Obviously the main reason I didn't want to come to court, is that I didn't want to wave goodbye again. This was always my problem with Jarmas—I didn't want him to be taken away but it was always on the cards though. I sat in the car for awhile and after about an hour of indecision, I got out of the car in the middle of a very crowded car park, dried my eyes and marched up to the main court house to find my MAN, so's I could stand by him.

Mat's case had not been heard yet and I found Pam opposite the courts and she told me the boys (boys being the operative word) had gone to the closest pub somewhere. I knew most of the pubs up this end of the City, so after checking a few we went to the Criterion and there they were. George had no money I know and John Boy was shouting him double scotches. Apparently the Duty Solicitor had already told him not to come back stinking of piss and here was his best mate helping him and I'm supposedly a complete bitch. HUH! Mat continued to skull as many scotches as he possibly could get down his gullet until it was time to go back to court.

When we did go back and much to John Boy's horror, I went downstairs in the court room with Mat and held his hand, as I maybe should have to start with. I really did love him I was just scared of yet another loss.

The judge entered and we all stood, we all bowed and then we all sat again. "Will Mat R. Cliff please be upstanding." He went through all the paper work and then said his piece. "I am not happy with your antics as a drunk, I'm not happy with anything I hear before me. As you, Mr M. R. Cliff are trying to better yourself and have a new life ahead of you in Nanango with this Lady, N.L.B. who has seen fit to forgive you, my sentence is six months probation. $2,500 to pay in restitution and if I see you again before me I'll throw the book at you".

Bang! Down went his hammer. Mat squeezed my hand so tightly at this moment—I was teary but not actually crying. I was glad for Mat and for his freedom. I was glad I still had a great big cuddly backhoe operator to come home with me. Well home, once we get to the property in Nanango. A whole new start, a new home, a new car, a new Family and a new area.

Things moved bloody swiftly after this and I guess it was mainly because there was a male attached. We went to a couple of car yards to trade in the shit box car I had bought on Macleay with the caravan. The people had led me to believe it would tow the van but it would not. I needed to find a 6 cylinder car. All the things I had specified that I wanted in a car were overlooked. All I wanted was a manual, station wagon with a good working stereo that wasn't white. What I got was a 1976 XB Holden Sedan that had a fucked radio, it was automatic and it was off white. Anyhow for $1,600 it was apparently a good deal and the best car in the place. It was the only one we were getting out of there with on that day, which would tow my caravan over the big hill where my new property was. The deal was done, the hands were shaken, money changed hands and I sat in the passenger seat. This was nice I s'pose,

This is nice isn't it? This is how it's meant to be.

My Father even said to me once, "You hang on to this one Nick." I was certainly going to try.

After we were all packed up at Pams' place with the caravan stuffed to the hilt with all my worldly possessions, plus the extra wood for chook pens etc, Off we went, the happy family with our new car and caravan and a new lease on life. The first problem arose on that very day because it was not me and my Mat, it was, Mat and his mate Jason and me and my kids. George had said that he would need Jason for a few days to help do any heavy work and to get a few things done on the block. Thinking back on it all I should have put my foot down right then and there. I should've said he could go buy his own car and caravan and his own fucking block with Jason if he so desired. So our new beginning was marred in my opinion and Should ofs don't work.

When we got to the property we set up the van in the best spot and got gas bottles, eskies and ice sorted out and a bit of a camp fire and a kitchen area outside, we sat back and relaxed round the fire and had a few beers. It was bloody freezing. The children were in their beds with hot water bottles and us three hovered together round the fire as close as you could be without burning your arse.

When Mat and I got out of our warm cuddly bed in the morning we discovered that fucking stupid Jason had burnt all the wood that Ray had given us to put up the chook pens and pig pens and park benches etc. He'd burnt the whole bloody lot. Mat went off his brain. "Do you think we'd cart all this, all the way up here (300 ks) to burn it all? There's eight acres of wood here you Stupid Brainless Twit and you've burnt the lot." Jason was a complete imbecile. He seemed so put out by Mat spewing at him that he went to the bus the next day and that was that.

Once again things cruised along nicely for awhile between us, but not so much on the Removal House side of things. The loan and house had all been approved but no one, at any point in time told me I had to have a $12,000 Bond for the Council. I had put $5,000 on the house, $5,000 on the block, $3,000 for the loan on the car and van which I had to pay out, and whatever I spent in between here and there. I definitely did not have $12,000 left for the council just to hold in their hot little hands. Next the boss at the Housing Co-op wouldn't release $20,000 of the $40,000 I'd borrowed for the house until the assessor had seen the house on the block. Naturally the House Removal Mob aren't going to part with their house, worth $18,000 until they've got the money. OH! FUCK!

I thought I'd lose all my money, and the house and block. This was a very stressful time. Then good ol' Lazza (my Dad) whacked up the twelve thousand for the Guarantee to the Council. It's just a guarantee to say I will finish the house up to NANANGO Shire expectations. If you had the 12 thousand in your pocket, you'd have enough to do what they expected. It's just another way for council and Government to make money and interest off all us poor bastards out here.

Joe Cliff (Boss, Lender) then wanted to lend me more money for a better house, and wanted me to put Mat-Mat on the contract. Dad said, "Yes, Nick you should do that because that would give him some responsibility and he wouldn't feel like a kept MAN". Personally I think any Australian Male doesn't care where it comes from as long as they've got IT and a beer in their hand.

I didn't want to borrow any more money and I didn't want to go in it together, because from my experience so far, you can't entirely trust a male to get his wallet out and pay his share, so go it alone Nick. After a few more phone calls and fuck ups Mat went off his brain at the Lender over the phone and Joe refused to speak to Mat or have any dealings with him again. Then of course Dad had to do a few calls on my behalf to Joe and fix up all the other shit and finally Mr. Joe Cliff sent out the money to the House Removal Mob.

It was all pretty bloody stressful for that entire month or two and Mat and I were stressed out to the max and were fighting a bit, as well. Whatever the case you just don't swear your head off at the bloke who may lend you $40,000. Simple rule, isn't it. I guess it's just the age factor, he was so mature in some ways and not in others.

Because money was becoming a problem, Mat wanted to go up north to an Island somewhere and get some crop of marijuana that he and some mates had put in. He wanted the kids and I to come with him as that would be a better cover. The happy family out fishing and holidaying. Naturally, I refused. No way am I putting my children or myself at that sort of risk. People with large crops often carry guns as well. That's nothing to do with the fact that it's illegal and the Police might be about. I did say to him he could borrow my car though, but that I'd have no part in the rest of it.

Next day was the day he wanted to go up North. There was a Hens' Party on for a friend of mine in Kingaroy and I was going to that, regardless of what he was doing. We both ended up going to town together, because apparently, all the blokes were having a drink at Lois's—my old friend; and then they were to go elsewhere while the Girls party went on . . . .

When we arrived, Mat asked for the biggest cup in the house and started drinking cheap wine, after cheap wine. All the fellas were inside watching the football and all the ladies, about 15 of them were outside congregated out the back around the barbie area with a bowl of punch. I'd brought my hair wrapping stuff with me so I could do a few hair wraps for the ladies. A hair wrap is a very thin plait wrapped round and round with different coloured threads and then followed by the appropriate matching beads.

Time went by and many drinks were drunk. I had, had a few by then too; but only the punch, which was mostly orange juice anyway. I decided to take the rotor button out of the car, because I know what

Mat is like on the piss. Any one could ask him to do a runner to the pub and he would, and in any condition. You know the type I mean. Jumps up between 10 or 20 people and goes, "Yeah, I'll do it," and unless he was three quarters pissed he would never do it, he'd let some other mug. It was my car too and I was only looking after my best interests, and his.

I continued on with my merry little hair wrapping duties and in the middle of doing Naomi's hair which was about 3 foot long, and Mat appeared. He staggered down the back ramp and across towards the car which was parked in the next paddock. I continued my hair wrap. He tried to start the car. A few times. I thought he'd just give up after a bit. Oh, no not Mat-Mat. He opened the bonnet next and obviously discovered—No rotor button! Raaaaahhhhhh! I pretended I didn't notice and continued with the hair. He came over to the ladies congregation then and straight towards me. He stopped leaned down as if to kiss me, which I thought he was gonna do, but he stooped down toward my face and bit into my eyebrow. He bit me as hard as he could. Ahhhhhh! I yelled out in pain and dropped the plait. Naomi realised what was happening and she stood up and punched him in the face causing him to release his painful clenching teeth off my eyebrow. Naomi was 6ft 4in and so was Mat. The punch set him back for one or two seconds and then he punched her back and then it was my turn again, and off the seat this time on which I'd been sitting doing the hair wraps.

While I collected myself off the deck he apparently swung punches at every chic in the place. He was like a mad man again. **Mad Mat.** Lois called for back up in the form of Atlas, who was at this point living on her block in a caravan.

Atlas came rushing from the van on another part of the property, but Mat had started up the chainsaw by then and it was just time to run . . . Run for your life. Everyone did. Everyone disappeared and George swung that chainsaw round like there was no tomorrow. After we'd all scattered from the barbie area he went to the gas bottles and tried to chainsaw through the pipes and then the bottles. He would have only blown his own fucking silly self to smithereens. I only know that part because I was the only silly one who ran inside the house and into a bedroom and was sneaking a look through parted curtains. I was frozen in position behind the curtain clinging to my first born and wondering where the fuck the 2nd one was. Sheer terror going through me, but I could not move away. Mat finally stopped trying to chainsaw everything in sight and stopped the chainsaw and ran back towards the car. My car, and then poured petrol all around it and then lit that up. I watched the ring of fire round my car for a time, then Mat ran back toward the house and threw the tin up the back ramp and into the back of the house.

From beyond, someone who obviously understood what the caper was; threw a rotor button out of his own panel van and yelled, "Here bloke—take it—and go. Mat went through the flames to the car, put the button in, got in the car and fucked off.

Slowly but surely people emerged from hiding spots up the road and round the yard, and me from the back room. Barry, the same bloke who threw the rotor button had already put out the fire in the laundry. One of the other wonderful ladies had my darling Ebony and everyone had come out of the ordeal at least with their life, but not completely unscathed.

Next scene was The Plodd, you know Noddy and Big Ears and Mr. Plodd—the Police. So for the next few hours all these nice ladies were questioned and made statements about the whole incident to the police. Poor bastards. I felt responsible even though I really hadn't done anything. I believe the statement bit went round about 20 people, who were initially out having a good time.

After all statements were collected everyone slowly left the scene and went to town, to various different pubs. There was only a few of us left. Lois my mate, and a couple of blokes. They were going to the pub too as soon as their statements were done. I was going to be left all alone with my 2 kids at the scene of the crime. Bullshit I am. I asked if I could go with them to the pub when the last one left, though I felt it was all my fault as usual.

"Yes Nick, was the reply. "You can't really stay here and wait for the crazed lunatic to come back."

Safety in numbers, they say.

The last of us went to the Kingaroy Pub. Most of the town already seemed to know what had happened and within minutes Mr. Crazed himself was paging me or Lois on the phone. Pete—the barman looked over at us, madly shaking our heads, and told him, no-one was here by that name. A further 10 minutes went by and another party member rang from the Club Hotel and told Lois Mat had just been caught and carted off to the lock-up.

Everyone breathed a sigh of relief and tried to enjoy the rest of the evening, and we could all relax in the knowledge that Mad Mat was safely out of harms way and could not come barging in through the door brandishing some form of violent weapon. Everyone else seemed to have gotten over the ordeal but I hadn't, the future to me looked bleak. I would have to forget about life with Mat and get used to the idea of going back to my little caravan alone. Lovely little caravan it was too.

I believe once again, that I don't quite remember the immediate few days after the drama. I still don't. I guess I just go numb for a time. After three days at Lois's the Plodd finally allowed me to have my car back. Apparently they were keeping it for evidence. What evidence? They had the bloke and they had the chainsaw and they let him go again. Why the fuck they needed my car or my chainsaw I'll never know.

Out to Lakes Estate we went, the two kids and the Mumma. I was sort of glad to get out of Lois's place. I try not to outstay my welcome, just sometimes we can't help it. At the same token, going home didn't look too thrilling either. All I had at this point was eight acres, one 18ft caravan with a very bodgey annexe and the HX that I mentioned earlier. *No tank, no toilet, no pool, no pets and I ain't got no cigarettes.*

Truly though I had a large esky which was our bath as well and 2 x 5 gallon drums for water and one dog with seven puppies.

On the way out there it started to piss down and I mean piss down. I was glad to have my car back and glad to be driving home. As I drove on and it continued to piss down all I could think of was that silly song., then it came on the radio. *"I thought it would rain the day you went away."* I was bawling and the wipers were working hard and the kids were asleep and right then the car died. GREAT. I almost fell completely to pieces—but no one noticed—so get it together Nicky and work out what to do now. A very kind unsuspecting neighbour came by and asked me if I was Ok. Well it was bleedin' obvious to me but we'll give him the benefit of the doubt and accept a lift to his home and phone and then ring the RACQ.

After many fuck arounds between the RACQ and the directions to where we are, etc. (and I had no idea where I was) The RACQ finally found Wally's house and then we all went down the end of Wattle Camp as I now know it and Mr. RACQ got the car going again in about 3 seconds, the smart arse. God I hate that. The kids were at the house with Wally's wife for that time and I picked them up on the way through and went home. *Home, Home on the range where there's nothing to laugh at, at all.* Went to bed very tired and very drained of energy.

This must be it.

CHAPPIE 12

INTERLUDE FOR ME AGAIN

Did heaps then—keep busy Nick—keep busy. I used to jog round the eight acres every morn' for awhile. I lost heaps of weight and I was pretty fit and happy. Stuart started school the next week and I used to have to drive over the two hills to take him to the school bus. On the same spot were all the letter boxes to the whole street. It was amazing who one can meet on a trip to the local letter box. I met my next door neighbour, Karen. She was great—a new friend. I'm sure it's hard to picture all this so I'll have to describe it betterer. Later.

I thought no one lived here but me and the lov-erly neighbors and then on one fine sunny morn' three kids appeared from the dense bushland and tapped on the side of the van. When I appeared, bleary eyed, in the doorway the kids said, "Can Stuart come out to play." Isn't that lovely? I was pretty spun out but was glad to see other kids in the area and Stu with a mate. So there were other signs of humans about and I didn't have concussion when I bought the place, after all.

It was still freezing time in Nanango and there were still the argie bargie with the co-op I was borrowing off. I believe my Father was

WRONG about getting extra money and making Mat someone on the papers and getting more money, and giving him responsibility, don't you? So I'm glad I bloody well didn't and it was finally, finally after three months of living in a humpy and showering maybe twice a week if ya lucky, time for the house to arrive. YaHoo!

I invited my sister to come up and watch the house arrival and to stay the weekend. She was pretty stressed about the Mat situation, but she came anyway. We both stayed in Nanango Town, that night at an old friend's place. Because we'd had a few the night before, we woke sort of late and I got in a dilemma about getting the 20ks before the house arrived. After all, some one's gotta tell them where to put the bleedin' thing.

I dashed off to the garage for the usual ice and gas for the stove in the caravan and there it was, in all it's glory—My little house. Excellently, excellent! I couldn't believe it was here and right in front of my eyes. The truck driver and his off-sider and the police escorts etc. were all breakfasting in the diner. I got my bits and pieces and dashed **baaack** to Sue's place to get my sister and, away. They must have been flying because they'd left the diner and were nowhere in sight by the time we got to the main drag again. We finally caught up to them on a little bridge over the Lee Baker Creek, because they had to jack the house up a bit to get across. I had the camera then and took a few shots of it all. We got held up again where a large tree, which they had to **ch-ain-saw** was blocking our path. More photos here. Then up over the big hill, which was a huge 70 degree angle that goes on and on. You feel like you're going up on a roller coaster ride and then down, down, down the other side and then up again. It's actually not so steep on my side of the hill, but after all the hard work to get up the first one you've got a fair sort of run up for the second hill. But look OUT! It stops dead on the next hill which is my cul-de-sac.

All Mine.

My only slight concern at this present moment was whether the house was going to end up in Dot and Alan's front yard and not in mine. Then I remembered that Mat had put in a few pot plants before the chainsaw incident and I had been watering them just at the back of the annexe. Much to my relief the Police just went round the round-about and they were gone.

The block had been cleared the week before to make way for the house to go into position. It's a damn shame that it had pissed down for a solid week before this great day and the bleedin' house got bogged. Well, it was the truck that got bogged, silly, with the house on it. So close and yet so far.

For awhile it was panic stations, because I thought I'd have ta' cough up more of my money for a D7 or something to get the house out again. But it finally became unstuck and the procedure went on. The Drake removal mob lowered it to the ground and then the three blokes jacked it up bit by bit with humungus great jacks. As it went slowly up they slid in another 6 x 6, and worked in unison across the underneath of the house until the house finally reached about a metre or a yard. Probably whatever the council law is. After the last blocks went in the blokes were away up the driveway and gone.

It was just so excellent and I was ecstatic. No one else could really quite understand it but me. I'd done it. I got the bloody house to the bloody block, and I was putting a roof over the heads of two of my children now and no one else—apart from ten men from Drake Removals, helped me. Not physically, financially and last but not least, mentally. I'm quite lucky to be still out of an asylum at this rate. Sometimes all this shit makes ya stronger and sometimes it can be the end of you. Me—it makes stronger.

I was just cruising along now. I had a home again and now I had 8 acres as well, instead of only a quarter of one. I only went in to the Kingaroy town once a week at this point in time to save on funds, but I nearly always went to Lois's because she was one of me old mates and we all need someone to talk to other than three and nine year olds all the time. I usually had one or two beers on my visit maybe three, but once again I always got home and now that there was one out there that was even betterer!

This was a time I realised even more why I had wanted a manual car. I knew already, but when the kids are watching the Tely on a 12 volt battery, well, they'll only get 1 hour's worth or the car won't start in the morning and we can't even push the bastard down the hill either but that is blatantly obvious. I was still carting water too, at this point, but I'd managed to collect about six five-gallon drums from the local pubs. They buy cleaning solutions and stuff like that and usually just throw away the drums. I could just squeeze five of these drums on the back seat and Ebony in the front. Stuart was at school and the boot was always full of shopping on the weekly trip in. It was a really amusing time. I ripped the fridge and stove out of the caravan and reconnected it in the house. I wasn't actually s'posed to move in to my own house until the council said so anyway, but I did get a second just before the removal blokes left to find out if it was safe to walk round in, or to do a few jobs.

"Move in if ya like, it's as safe as houses," said the bloke.

We each had a mattress on the floor and I also had an old 2 x 2 seater and another single seater that Pam's neighbour had given me and that was about it. I did still have a few bits and pieces on Macleay at a friend's house which I'd have to get at a later date when I could afford to hire a trailer. I had all the usual bullshit, like pots and pans, plates and cups etc etc. just no fridge and no proper stove, well no power anyway. The house did have a decent stove and a hot water system in it, as well as shower, bath, toilet, laundry tub and full kitchen with sink and drainers, just no water connected. This particular house had come from the Gold Coast somewhere and it had three sets of French doors along the front, so therefore I would need three sets of steps or a verandah for a start. The three sets of steps would be a lot cheaper, so that would have to do for now. One thing about a removal house is that you get the whole lot in one hit, there's no worries about getting all those aforementioned items like stove and kitchen cabinets done. What you maybe don't realise or at least I didn't realise initially was the much bigger extras, like for example bloody rain water tanks, power poles and connections, phone lines dug up and put down the block from the top, gates, fencing and fire breaks around the place.

It makes one realize that water is a necessity for everyday life, but I already knew all about rain water tanks anyway from Macleay times. The water tanks on Macleay were already there and attached to the house thankfully. I had a few bucks so I ended up purchasing my first tank off some locals who were moving.

"How much?" I asked.

"You can have it for the same as we paid," said the woman. "Which was a five dollar scratchy."

"Done!" I said.

Next came the problem of getting the bastard home. So it was beg, borrow or steal a trailer off some nice person.

This all came together without any setbacks and then I got a load of sand in the same borrowed trailer to rest the tank straight on to. Water was priority 1, and the next job was to concrete the bloody thing because it had quite a few rust spots in it. I heard lots of different ways of doing this particular job and lots of recipes for the cement mix, I chose my father's recipe. (mmmmmmmm)

It was 5 shovels of sand to one cement, and when the mixer's full add 1\2 a cup of Bondcrete. The next step is to wire chicken-wire inside the tank to help hold the concrete together.

So I naturally did all of the above and the girl next door, Karen, helped. Karen was great, she was a single mother of two sons, Mat and Joel, and lived just over the hill. We used to help each other all the time with different projects. After the job was done I wrote in the bottom of the tank, "Nicky and Karen were here—who needs men." Well when the water carter, Potter Managan came out to fill it, the bloody thing leaked like a sieve. It was just like one of those cartoons, where someone gets shot at 20 thousand times and the blood spurts out in every direction. Luckily I have a sense of humour otherwise I'm sure I would have broke down and cried, but I just laughed. What else could I do. Have another go, ya mug. Potter seemed as though he felt a bit bad, but he had done his job and should be paid. After all it's not his fault that my bodgy tank leaked. Seems Dad was wrong again for the second time in his whole life.

The next week I got a **goo-gun** and some plastic silicon stuff and went around every single hole that I had put in it to hold the chicken wire, then would you believe, **it rained**. I didn't even have to ring Mr Water Carter again and the tank held too, so we had water for the first time at our new house. We just had no pump and no connections to the taps. Next step, Pump. Another good bargain here—I got an automatic pump off a bloke I'd just started cleaning for, for $25.00 and they cost about $250.00 new. I had a few bits and pieces of rainwater pipe to run from the house to the tank but had to wait another week to be able to afford the other pipes to connect pump to house.

Then was the big one; **Power.** I wanted the house a fair way back on the block so now the power was gonna be a fair price too. The house ended up being about 100 metres back so it was going to cost $1,600 and as far as I'm concerned it was well worth every cent. Everyone was saying I had my priorities wrong but then they're not living here alone with 2 kids and no power, no tely, no hot water, no lights and once again, No Tely. I really love me tely and the kids missed it a lot too. All the bright sparks around the place said "buy tanks" priority ONE, but I had one tank and that will do for now. The place had been put on concrete stumps now too, so that was $2,200 and the money was getting short now and I wanted power.

"Let there be power," said I and there was Power, well after the dollars changed hands.

It was so great, you've no idea how wonderful it really was. I could finally have a shower in my own home and with hot water too. I s'pose you think I did not shower at all for the past couple of months, but up until this time we'd been using the shower room but with one of those black solar bags that you get for camping. I'd fill it up each day and leave it in the sun and we'd all have a quick splash together in the late afternoon while it was still warm. Sounds like rollicking fun doesn't it! Now I could also cook a proper meal in the stove and wash up after in hot water, lovely hot water. The kids could watch tely till their hearts content and there was no messing about with extra long jumper leads each and every afternoon. Neither was there the worry of not being able to start the car because I'd let them have extra TV time. Things were looking up and everything was slowly but surely coming together in the fashion of a real home.

I had made a few friends around the area to have occasional drinks with, so I wasn't toooo lonely. I still had Lois in town as well and stayed in at her place sometimes so's I could go to the Pub or Club or something. To tell the honest, I was pretty happy with myself at this point in time. I had achieved most of my goals for the year. I sold the house and got off the Island. I got a block. I got a house and put it on the block and now we have power, as well! Pretty damn clever, if I do say so myself.

Then Mat started writing to me from jail. Not that I answered him of course. He got 4 four years altogether for his little tantrum and he would probably end up doing about a year if he was a real good boy. He was sorry as well. He was very sorry in fact and he wanted another chance. HUH! I still did not write back. Life went on and I got a few more things done off the list the Council had given me.

The house still had to be painted inside and out, the anchor bolts had to be tied down to the stumps, the septic had to be done and the grey water outlet and grease trap. Then there was only to paint the roof, put drains in the bathroom and laundry and splash back behind the tub and a few more water tanks to make it up to 5000 gals. And that was all.

Instead of doing all these things I was lying on my bed one day reading a Mind Power Book. I'd been reading it for the past week and now I thought I'd put it into action. I was deeply thinking about Jarmas and wishing him to me, wishing and tuning in and calling out, "Jarmas come to me." Jarmas come to me". Next minute there was a loud knock on the door, which scared the shit out of me. I jumped up and went out to the front door and here in the doorway is a tall fairly rough looking, bearded wonder; arm outstretched to introduce himself. I did the same.

"Jarmas's me name. How 'ya going?"

I was in shock, but managed to introduce myself.

"I just came to see if you had any work that needs doing."

"Well yes." I answered. Heaps and heaps of work Jarmas but no dollars though, so I'll have to do it myself." Then he asked me if I smoke, to which I said yes. Then I invited him in for coffee and cones. After we got to know each other a bit we had a couple of wines. Then he asked how much water I had. To which I replied, "bugger all again now". (it hadn't rained again since the tank had half filled with water, and now it was empty again) So Jarmas invited me for a drink at his place and a shower as well and I accepted due to the fact I hadn't had a shower for a few days now.

It was all very kosher—he had 2 solar shower bags the same as mine, and he filled them right up and at perfect temperature and hauled them up to the very high beam with his huge muscles. Not like me who had to fight tooth and nail to get mine up to the ceiling and mine was only 1\2 full. He also had a blanket hanging around this old bath tub so's no one could see. Ebony had a shower with me.

When we emerged, there was another couple there having a wine too, so I stayed for awhile and we all had a happy little evening. James, as he seemed to be mostly known, was so much like Jarmas it wasn't funny. He even had the same dimples. Who really needs another Jarmas. The first one was really more than enough. So back home I went with all my little problems.

Now that I'd met a few people in town and a few people out here, I thought I'd have a barbie or a sort of house warming at home. I had to keep busy and keep my mind occupied and keep my foolish mind off Mat. Lois came out to the barbie and brought a bloke with her named Lee, he was really nice and he lived out this way too, just in the next street in fact. I was getting a good group of friends out here now, there was no need to feel lonely. Lee, or Hippy Lee, as I came to know him, was saying to me that I should definitely not forgive Mat. Not ever. I was telling him all about the chain-saw bit at some stage and he said that once a man is violent toward a woman it never changes, it only gets worse. True Story. I had not planned on giving Mat a second chance anyway, well not really. He wanted to do Home Detention here and I was seriously thinking about it, but not sure. He wouldn't be allowed to drink anyway, for at least another year, but would I do the same; probably not. So the decision was made. I finally wrote back and told him it would never work again—too much water under the bridge. Bye Bye!

My parents came up for a weekend and it was really great to see them. Dad was so proud of me at this point in time, though he never said it, I just know he was. He was on my case too, on a regular basis about how all the jobs were going towards the final on the house. Slowly, slowly Dad, but it's getting there, was my usual answer. I had six months to finish all the council's list of stuff for Dad to get his $12,000 back without it incurring any costs to him. (STRESS)

Dad did a few odd jobs while he was up here though and gave me a lot of good pointers of how to do different things. I would still listen to him even though he stuffed up on the recipe for fixing a holey tank. One night while my parents were up, Hippy Lee came round. I went out to see what he wanted and he was here to invite me out to share a bottle of Scotch with him at a friend's place. I asked Mum if she minded if I went for a while and she said go for it. I didn't know him all that well but a night out of the place and away from the kids would be a nice change, the bottle of Scotch was just an added bonus. We ended up driving around the Estate for awhile looking for his mates who weren't home. Then he said he'd take me round to Margret's place, a lady who only lived in the next street over from him. He also told me she was a White Witch and was very interesting. We stayed there for most or all of the bottle, and I had yet another new friend, who was by the way, very interesting as Hippy had said. He dropped me home at about midnight like a good little boy would and said, "I'd like to see you again, if I may?"

I thought he was very cruisey and casual, a nice dresser, he didn't mind a drink or a smoke; yeah, I'll see him again.

CHAPPIE 13

HIPPY LEE AND THE FIVE PEOPLE I HADN'T MET BEFORE

After that night, Lee came round quite regularly to see me, often to give me a hand doing some horrible job I couldn't quite manage on my own. Then after only a few short weeks, I felt completely swept off my feet by this fellow. He bought me drinks and flowers all the time and he bought me lingerie and a few dresses. He told me all the time how gorgeous I was and how I should dress up to look good and to take more pride in my appearance. He wasn't being nasty, he just reckoned if you've got it flaunt it, and as far as he was concerned, I had it, whatever it was. I actually listened to him too, I dressed myself up a bit better and a bit more often and I lost weight. I felt so great with him around.

When I told him one day that I wasn't intending to stay here forever and that it was just a stepping stone. He said, "No Nicky, darling, I'll make it so beautiful here that you'll never want to leave."

He loved me and I felt loved too. I really like that, to know you're loved, to be told you're loved and to feel it. I was the Queen and I was gorgeous. Lil' ol' me. I was in Love. I was completely nuts about him. I wanted to do everything and be everything for him. I couldn't wait for him to arrive and I missed him every moment he was away. In hindsight, my big attraction was his teeth. They were worse than mine, so any time I smiled, it was OK.

A few weeks later I had a Divorce Party to go to on Macleay Island. Lee said he'd miss me heaps and heaps while I was away, I knew I would miss him just as much so I asked him to come with me. He was really wrapped in that idea. He suggested it would be cheaper to go in his car because it was four cylinder and a station wagon as well, which is better when you're carrying eskies and tents and stuff. He offered to drive as well. How wonderful, it's nice to have someone else drive me around again for a change. I think Lee was enjoying his trip to the Islands. It was a whole new experience for him.

When we got to Lisa's she gave us her bedroom for the night. This was pretty unusual, but I s'pose I usually went visiting on my own. I don't really remember much of that party except that Lee was there, and that I was happy. Very happy.

Next day, Hippy and I went up to Mum and Dad's place. Actually they picked us up from Lisa's which is halfway up the Island. The Island is 5 miles long and about a mile wide in the widest part. My parents lived up the far end from the Jetty, in the flash section. I used to be in the middle too—not far from Lisa's—she reckoned she could hear Jarmas and I fighting in the old days. Anyhow forget him, back to Hippy Lee. Well here we are at Ma and Pa's house, in the bar of course, and Hippy Lee says to my own Mother, "You'll never have to worry about your daughter again, I'll look after her and treat her like a Queen."

I was going to Marry this one, I could **tell.** This is him. He is THEE one. He was gonna look after me. Oh how wonderful. At last! Someone whose going to look after me. Like my Father looked after my Mother. Someone to organise things and to take care of the bigger dramas in everyday life.

The whole weekend went extremely well and both Lee and I were just happy to have each other. Lisa was happy for me to have finally found a good bloke and was glad to see me in love again after the last few years of hell. I told Lisa that Lee and I had already talked of marriage and that I was intending to wear a gorgeous red dress that Lee was going to pick out and pay for. It was all pretty mad really, but it felt right. I did not think of Jarmas so much, if at all these days. Lee completely occupied my mind and my days and nights. **Nice-lee, sweet-lee, happy-lee, Hippy-Lee.** Everything was perfect. I wanted the whole world to know I was in love with Lee. He met all my family and friends over the next few months, we went everywhere together. None of my mates seemed to like him terribly much though. Oh well who cares. I'm the one spending the rest of my life with him.

Da-dada-der-dan-dan da da!

ATTY'S FUNERAL

In between all this happiness and bliss an old mate of mine died, that is to say he's no longer with us, no longer here on this planet. Firstly I'll have to describe Atlas to you at great length, this is so you can meet the person, and understand why I felt I had to be there at his funeral.

I met him years ago. Mother Duck, who was disgusted in him, first brought him to my attention. Mother had bought my sister and I a brand spanking new lounge each—pull out lounge type model. A few weeks after this fact, she visited my sister's house, and there plonked on Linda's new lounge bed, was the very disgusting, drunk Atlas. Some people called him, "Road Maps" as well (Because his eyes were so bloodshot). He was rather a large fellow, probably from working out in the Jail House, he was covered in tats and usually half pissed. He was also the type of bloke that would wear his clothes for days and days and then he'd turn them inside out and go another day or so. You can understand Mum's horror on their first meeting.

One of the first few times I had met him was on a particular day when Kelly and D were at my place at Bowen Hills having a few Magnums of Summer Wine. Lois rang and said "Nicky you best get your arse over here and sort out your silly sister. Apparently, Lyn and Atty had been drinking Datura. How the fuck ya spell that I don't know, but they were both off the planet.

Well bloody hell, here's Kelly and I half pissed, but decided to go anyway. Kelly was driving, her new Gallant, that she'd had for 2 days. She had the Magnum of wine between her legs, I was blabbing on about how I should probably get a loan so I could buy a decent car like this and then cruncha! Kelly ran up some blokes arse and then leapt out and abused the shit out of him. God it was funny, looking back on it all.

When we arrived at Malinda's, the pair of idiots were, wandering about the flat stark staring naked. They had washed their hair in Vaseline and had also been scribbling all over each other in Niko Pen. Kelly was spinning out about her car and was on the phone to her mother, who was the insurer of the car we'd last been driving. Malinda headed off out the front door. I thought it was all highly amusing and continued to drink another Magnum (with Kelly's help of course). Malinda and Atty finally ran out of drug induced hysteria and both passed out.

Our job is over now, now that they're both asleep, so Kelly and I went off out on the town, and she was driving like a maniac too. She was saying, "I've already fucked me new car now, so I don't give a shit anymore." We did make it home though, once again.

The next amusing story on the beautiful Atlas was the time he sold his car. We were all going to an engagement Party that night and Atlas the Stupe, had two thousand dollars in his top pocket. Nothing was too much if Atlas wanted to Party. God only knows how much he spent, but I know for a fact that he bought a box of J.D. **TO START WITH.** He shared that lot round the party and by morning he went back to get another, and the Publican said "Sorry Mate you've bought us out." He was a complete lunatic, He was lunaticified, which was one of his many silly words. He was great. A laugh a minute, but that's from a mate, a fella drinker, if you will.

I nearly fell off my chair, on another occasion with Atty Poo Bags, as he came to be known by Lyns. A whole mob of us were sitting round the table at the ISLAND House and as usual. Atlas was plastered to the eyeballs. He started mixing drinks. I mean mixing drinks. Like, there were about 7 different drinks on the table and he was pouring everyone's dregs all together and then sculling that. As you can well imagine, beer mixed with bourbon and coke and then Bailey's with milk is gonna curdle. UUUUgggggghhhhhh! It was revolting, He drank it though and held it down, at the same moment he was holding what was left of his carton, on his lap, and guarding it with his life. All the while rolling his eyes round in his silly head and cackling with glee.

Then—up it came and straight into the half empty carton (or half full) situated on his left leg. I was sitting on his right, thank Christ, and all I could do was laugh. I have never laughed so much, before or after. Ya had to be there. The rest of the crew seemed to move back in slow motion towards the back and front door. I just sat next to him in hysterics. I was glued to the chair, because if I did move I would have wet myself. Just a day in the life of ATLAS and his antics.

He asked me to marry him once too. It was just after my sister had left him and I guess he was feeling rather lonely, needless to say I knocked him back and who wouldn't after being proposed to over the phone. The Bloody Cheek!

So all in all I guess I'd known Atlas about 10 years and when he died I felt so sad at the loss of a Kindred Spirit. I felt I had to be there to say goodbye. I just wanted one last beer, one last session with him and this was as good as it got. I absolutely had to be there.

Lee was being Mr Wonderful and offered to mind the Kids, while I went down to Brisbane. My car was out of order so I decided I'd have to hitch. Lee dropped me on Nanango Highway just past the last

Petrol stop and on I went. It didn't seem funny to me at the time, that he should do this. I was just doing what I wanted as per, and he was allowing it. He was just so easy to get along with.

I got a lift in about three minutes and the bloke was going to Brisbane and straight past the road that the Crematorium was on. We chatted away for the two hour trip and he ended up dropping me right outside the place. I was hours early then because I gave myself an extra two and a half hours just in case I didn't get a lift. Oh well good time to sit and think.

Atlas had sort of O.D.ed but not really. He was all alone and had some sort of drugs and fell down a short flight of stairs and it was the way he fell that actually finished him off, because he'd cut off his wind pipe and there was just no one there to help him up. Sad, sad, sad. Seems silly but I always expected him to run into a tree one way or another; motorbike, car, truck, plane, not that it makes any difference to the out-come, nor would it make anyone feel any better about it.

I hadn't ever met Atty's adoptive family, but they obviously loved him. We all did, all that were there. They did a beautiful job on the words and poetry, it was all quite tear-jerking as they say in the movies. Unfortunately the complete bitch that Atlas spent his last year or so with, leapt up during his sister's speech and yelled out "What a load of fucking shit. Atlas hated the whole lot of you." I wanted to go slap her down but she was about two aisles over and 4 four rows back. Someone shut her up, quick smart. Jesus Christ! Unbelievable that a person could be such a **bitch at a time like this,** to any of the family. I have always blamed her anyway because he was totally off the shit and had been for years, until she found him again. Atty used to be a pimp (her pimp) years before and she was apparently in love with him and found him again—worse luck.

Goodbye Atty Poo Bags.

After two beers at the pub next door to the crematorium with a whole lot of the old school chums it was time to go. Malinda was there. I think she was more hurt by it than she let on, but she'd just

not long had her second child and didn't have time for pain and grief.
(or more beer) I had to leave with her I s'pose, after all she is my sister.
All I wanted to do was drink. I wanted to drink at the Crematorium.
I thought everyone in the whole place should have sculled at least one
largie of V.B. in Atty's Honour. I went back to Malinda's for a while
and then Cess came home and it was all quiet and Happy Families
style. I had to get out of here. I rang Pam. Jim was there and he came
immediately to pick me up and to take me where ever I wanted to be.

The Sundowner Hotel at Beenleigh was where all the ol' mates
had cruised on to. They were all there. We drank many largies. Stayed
till stumps. Cried a little and laughed a lot. He was such a funny bloke.
Jimery and I both stayed a Lois's at Beenleigh for the night. We started
up again the next day too and drank into oblivion, again.

I remembered about 5pm that next day, that I had a lift home to
Nanango with the bloke I'd hitched down with. I rang his mobile and
told him I wasn't ready and would have to find my own way home.
Then I rang Lee and told him I was sorry for fucking up and I couldn't
get home till tomorrow which was payday. He said, "No problems
at all Nick, take as long as you need. I love you. Hope to see you
tomorrow then Darling." Yep, bye. CLUNK. And back to the beer.
Jim was a real Champ to have around for an unhappy chappie. Kept
us all laughing. All good things must come to an end though and after
two days it was definitely time for the Nicolaza to get her arse home.
But how?

Hitching in to the big smoke is one thing, but hitching out is a
completely different scene. I definitely wasn't up for it. Jimery still had
Ewans' car and was willing to steal or borrow it for a week or so.

"No way," I said. "I'll be right, I'll get my own way home."

You wouldn't believe it. You couldn't believe it unless you were
there. I walked out of Gazelle Villas, where Lois lived and directly
opposite was a Volvo for sale for $400 bucks. I went over with Jim and
told the bloke I had only $300 for the car and $20 left for petrol to get
home to Nanango. He took the ONO sign off and said. "It's yours
Baby, and I've never seen you before in my life." No problems. It even

had a battery in it and he left the plates on. Ye Ha! Started her up, paid the bloke and went opposite for the $20 fuel.

Bye-bye Jimrey. I parted with him at the toll roads. Go west young girl and he went back to Pammy's. Bloody hell that car went like a pearla. I was cruisin' along at about 100kms all the way home and she didn't miss a beat. Everyone always whinges about Volvos and Volvo drivers but I reckon they're fucking OK. OK!

Lee was well impressed when I got home with a new car. How clever I am. We took off just where we left off before I went away for Atlas' funeral. I was so glad to be home and Lee was so glad to have me back with him.

One evening shortly after this, we went out with Karen and her new boyfriend. It was an all night thing. A verandah party or a balcony party, something like that. It was a huge party and they even had a couple of bands there. At some stage of the night, Lee said, "Come on, I'm off to bed now." (we were sleeping in his car) "Not me, I'm partying and I'm not missing this band for anyone."

He seemed a bit pissed off, but went off to the car anyway and I stayed up most of the night. I slithered in beside him in the early hours. I snuggled up to him and he got up shortly afterwards. I guess he must have been more pissed off than I realized. I was hurt but I tried not to let it worry me too much and besides, I was still pissed.

Heath and Karen were coming up for Roast Pork that night as well so when we got home about lunch time I had to clean up a bit and get the dinner going. First I lit the wood stove and put the water on to wash up and then plonked on the lounge to rest while that happened.

"Fuck it, if you're going to sleep, I'm going to bed," said Lee. And off he went. I cried a little and then I just got on with it as you would. Washed up, cleaned up and got the dinner going. Lee slept on. Karen, Heath and the kids arrived about 5pm. They wondered where Lee was and I explained to them, he seemed pissed off with me and went to bed.

He never did get back up that night either. He left me to play alone with my neighbors. It seemed to be a sort of punishment, for the night before. I did take a dinner in to him and he just said, "Do you really expect me to eat that shit, Nicky." He left it on the tray on the dresser.

I could not understand it. What's happening here? I don't know where this is coming from. This wonderful man I love so much is just really being nasty to me. I went in to have a shower, and I'd just got undressed and turned on the $25.00 pump and then the shower. Two seconds later, Lee burst into the room and I just covered myself up. He'd never actually seen me before standing stark staring naked. I was horrified. I was still trying to cover up and he was screaming at me. I mean screaming at me, at the top of his lungs. I didn't understand what he was on about. Then it finally twigged that I should have turned the taps on before the pump. With all the obscenities and abuse he carried on with, I couldn't quite figure out what his problem was.

I stood there in shock and horror. Absolute horror. This wonderful bloke—once again was getting scary, real fucking scary. I had my shower then and by the time I got out he was sorry. He was so sorry for yelling at me and he explained that he felt real low after a big weekend and he gets real touchy after too much of a good thing. He was oh so sorry. Etc. etc.

I felt differently now and I was worried. I was very worried. He had a streak and a real agro streak, but different to anything I'd seen before. He seemed to be super sweet, **OR NOT**. Any how I was keeping a serious eye on this. I didn't feel any less love for him and the horror seemed to pass and fade and life went on, as it does.

A couple of days later I was moaning about having to sort out a back-hoe operator about getting my septic in and informed Lee, that I was going down to Eddie's to organize that. Eddie is one of the locals of the longest standing or the oldest bloke here, I'm not sure which, but he definitely knew it all and had the longest beard. I guess after living on Macleay Island for all those years, ya sort of get to know who would be most likely to know what's going on around the place and who's the cheapest. On Macleay, it was Bill and he knew where to hire anything and most of it was from him. He knew exactly where to put his finger on just about anything one might want. Around here it was Eddie that seemed to fit the Bill so to speak. So naturally he's the bloke I was going to see.

Well! Did that hit a bad spot or what.

"You're not going down to Eddies at all, Bitch. I'll organize the plumbing and septic tanks. I'm the man here and I'll take care of all that needs doing."

Unfortunately he was yelling at the top of his lungs at the time and also holding me by the throat. He was also salivating like a rabid dog and spitting his words into my face with more venom than a black mamba. After a bit of domestic violence (which by the way I'm used to) I escaped and got the kids and went to Eddie's as planned. Eddie and his wife were having a few drinks and welcomed me in to their humble abode. I wasn't there very long, just long enough to get the info about the plumber bloke, and to have a beer, maybe two, and then back home again.

When I got back home, Lee was gone and I was relieved to say the least. After all—it's my house and it's my fucking plumbing and my problem. Me and the kids all went to bed in my bed like we used to in the caravan. Like after Mat-Mat was gone and we all needed a cuddle—mostly me.

Next morning when the Back-Hoe turned up so did Lee. He got there just before, and made all his apologies and promises. I told him I couldn't cop any more violent shit and reminded him of how we met and the fact that he had said, "Once a basher, always a basher". He was crying and telling me how sorry he was and that whatever had happened between us now, he still wanted to do everything for me because he loved me **soooooooo** much.

As you've probably gathered from the last ten chappies, I don't have much of a clue on property or building, OK. Lee was directing the Back-Hoe bloke where to go and what to do. Obviously the operator had some clue of what he was doing with his ever so large machine. So he got the grease trap and septic and that done. Then he proceeded on to dig a large hole at the side of the house, which was to be the underground car park, underneath the large room which Lee was gonna build. But as you and I both know by this stage of the book that this fucker wasn't gonna be round for all that long. I doubted very much that he would have got the job done anyway.

He was just another male who saw what he wanted and took advantage of the situation to the hilt. What's new? Nothing at all is new. It's just the same ol' same ol'. All I had to do was to get rid of him out of my face now. I told him straight up that day. "Lee I can't go on with this any more. You've scared me with yelling and screaming in my face and I've been through it all before and I can not go on with it again."

He finally left saying that he'd make it up to me and he would get me back and we were so right for each other that things would work out in the end. He still came round on a regular basis after that and I still had some feelings for him too, though one of the feelings was **FEAR.**

During this time I had the council people here to check the house for the final. Mr Kerry Mercer, the building inspector said, "Everything is just about passable Nicky, except you'll have to get that big hole at the side filled in or the house will fall in it. Oh my God! All these helpful arseholes and now I've gotta get someone to fill the hole in again.

Anyhow when the lovely Lee came round the next time I told him just that. He had dug a big hole in the wrong spot and now it has to be filled in before the final. I was actually out on the block while saying this. Next minute he dragged me back to the house saying, "You've gotta ring, it's your house" so I've gotta ring the bloke. I've gotta ring it's my house and my problem. He dragged me by the hair for about quarter of an acre or something, who'd know. Then when we got to the house he threw me on to the stairs. It's a pity there were no stairs. They were just still the large blocks that used to chock the house up. The fellas from Drakes left me enough to make steps at the front. Thanks fellas.

When I felt apart like a blithering idiot, on these particular steps, he got even more pissed off. So he picked me up off the steps and threw me into the lounge room on my back. I was winded, terrified and in shock. I couldn't possibly move. I remember this bit clear as a bell. I was lying there in shock and he jumped. He jumped up high once or twice, maybe three times and he also landed again, each time his two boots got closer to my head. All the time he was screaming.

I honestly thought my heart was gonna leap right out of its casing. I stopped breathing for a bit but that was only the seconds before the steel caps hit the deck either side of my head. After they landed I seemed to be able to draw breath again. Thank Christ. I laid there for quite some time. I just felt like I never wanted to move again, even if I could and I also felt like if I did move I could get the big boots all over again. Next thing he was yelling at me. "Get up. Get up you fuck wit. You're not hurt, I hardly touched you."

I was still lying there teeth clenched and terrified to move. I decided though, that if I didn't get myself off the floor and try to look normal I would cop more shit. It didn't work very well though. I'm not a very good actress, and once you've told a bloke that you're not happy any more, it's pretty hard to convince them otherwise.

We sat at the dining room table for an hour or so and I was just trying to tell him I needed some space and I did still love him, but I just needed some time alone because of my own problems with life and men. He knew I did not love him anymore. I'd already said. He dragged me up the hallway then. I thought he just wanted to take me to bed (where I didn't want to go) but I was wrong. He actually wanted to lay me to rest. He wanted a double suicide, but it's not a double suicide unless both people want to do it, otherwise it's **MURDER.**

As usual the bath was full of water because I always kept it for flushing the toilet or watering the garden. Lee got me as far as the bathroom door and when he reached up for the hair drier, I realized what was going through his fucked up brain and grabbed the sides of the doorway and grabbed at everything I could. My last screams of, "Please, please don't Lee, pleeease don't do it, I'm not ready. I'm not ready to go yet." He stopped.

"Do you want me to stay?" he said. What the fuck am I to do, let him finish us both off or say, "Yes." Well guess what, I said yes. "I do want you to stay Lee, we can work things out I'm sure."

The kids had been in bed for a while and didn't have to witness all this shit, thank God for small miracles. Lee took me in to the bedroom then and we sat on the bed and had a large joint together. Lee tried to do the sex bit on me and I was still so completely terrified, I didn't know what to say.

"Oh please just hold me Lee, just hold me tightly tonight, I'm so tired now." That seemed to be OK with him and we both went to sleep.

Things always seem better in the light of day. Stuart went off to school and the day started out pretty normally, well, as normal as could be expected with a complete maniac, schizo, nutcase. Well absolutely nothing seemed better or brighter, but the sun was up. I was cleaning up and Lee was looking for the rake, apparently to clean up outside. I could hear him swearing to himself—then he got louder and louder. "Where is that fucking rake, it was bloody well here last night. Where the fuck is it. Some fucking kid's probably moved it. Nicky(still yelling) your daughter has taken the fucking rake and I want it now!" He was at a deep low growl by this stage. Ebony looked terrified and rushed down the back to get it where she had been playing. Lee rushed after her to see if she could find it. When she came back dragging the rake, he started to run after her and I spotted them round the side of the house through the window. Lee had caught Ebony by the arm and was laying into her with open handed smacks. It was too much, too many, and too fucking hard. I screamed my lungs out and he stopped. Ebony bolted straight to me and I chucked her in the car which fortunately had the keys in it and we took off out of there at 100 miles an hour.

As far as I was concerned anyway, it was all over before this, I just didn't know how to get away from him or how to deal with him at all. He wasn't the bloke I met. I was ready for anything to happen on that day so I was quick to think when it did. I didn't know where I was going but I didn't care as long as the distance between him and me was getting further I was happy. As usual I didn't have hardly any money so I couldn't fuck right off to Brisbane. I decided to go to Big Bill's who was a good friend of Lois'. He welcomed me in and offered me a drink to calm the nerves. Kids were set up in front of a nice video and Bill's other flat mate organized us a bed in the lounge. I settled in for a wine and whinge session with Bill. He said, he did know Lee was a bit off tap, but the suicide bit was unexpected.

Anyhow none of that mattered any more, now I just had to get rid of him out of my house and out of my life. I knew this one was not going to be easy, because he was crazy. I thought he must really be a schizophrenic by this stage, though I didn't really know what schizophrenic was. I thought it was a good person and inside their head was Mr. Evil, Nasty Bastard.

I stayed at Bill's for the night and we drank. I didn't seem to get drunk though and I knew it wasn't gonna make me the usual happy drunk that I am because I was far from happy. I had been hit before and abused and all the rest, but no one is ever touching my kids but me. Their own Daddies aren't here and I'm the only one to discipline them at all. I'm their Mum and Dad. I will always be their Mum and Dad now. No one else seems to be capable of the Father figure too much any more, least of all Lee.

On we go regardless. I ring my place in the morning and Lee answered. "Hello."

"I want you out of there TODAY." I said.

"Don't worry Bitch I'll be gone." Clunk.

Uuummmmm! So do I go home or not? Have to, it's my home. It's our home and there's nowhere else to go. Back out to the farm house we went, and he was gone. His stuff too. I was so relieved but I was also scared shitless as well, because the bastard only lived in the next street. That was about 2ks away but, too close for comfort. I sat around nervously for the next two days. He did come up the hill and go round the cul-de-sac a couple of times but never drove in. Just enough to make me a complete nervous wreck.

CHAPPIE 14

INTERLUDE FOR ME

As it happened I was off to Pam and Ray's wedding that weekend so I was glad go get out of the place for a couple of days. A friend of mine offered to mind the kids so I could have a complete break from the whole of life, as I know it. Good stuff, time out for little Nicky.

I was very depressed about the whole deal and the fact that once again, I seemed to have picked a **violent, mixed up fuckwit from hell. Shit!** I had plenty to keep me occupied though, what with all that had to be done for Pammy's Wedding. For the past few days, though I was a nervous wreck. I'd been cooking madly the whole time. Making all sorts of pastries and a few other a la carte dishes, to take down to Brissy with me.

All the shitty music for Lovers played all the way to Pam's no matter which station I put it on. I cried a bit, but it's wise not to lose it while driving. "Snap out of it Nicky, just snap out of it." Deep breaths.

I was happy when I got to Pamalaza's. I always am. Her Ma and Pa where there, Ray of course, Russell the Big Brother and his wife and the odd cousin. I relaxed way back and had a bloody good night. We drank a little, laughed a lot and other than that we were flat out in the kitchen. I reckon between Pam, her Mother and I we made about 30 different chicken dishes (we still had access to cheap chicken) and about 30 other assortments of salads and pasta, as well as quite a few variations of deserts. We cooked and fucked around in the kitchen till about 3am and finally crashed.

Now for the big day—"**THE WEDDING**"

We all got up about 6am and back to the kitchen again to finish off any little frilly bits and then to pack it all into eskies and boxes. We packed up crockery, cutlery, linen and anything else one might want for a wedding table. As we got each box or esky ready they were passed to some bloke or other and transported to the reception room which was fortunately only a few K's up the road.

Pam was to be married at 3 o'clock in a lovely little park at Victoria Point, the reception to be held at the Football Club opposite.

After getting, most of the food organized, we had a short break for brekkie and cornflakes and then back at it again. The stereos had to go and all the alcohol and huge stacks of serving dishes; we just seemed to be flat out all morning. It must've been about one-ish that we all went up to the football club with the last few bits and pieces. After getting it all in the place, Pam, Ray and I stopped briefly and shared an expensive bottle of champers which I'd bought specially. It was a nice interlude, but it was over real quick. What a shame.

Pam had to rush off and do all the stuff that Brides do, like hair, nails, make-up etc. I felt a little bit sorry for Pam in many ways, she was so rushed off her feet all the night and most of the next day and was still rushing now. I was thinking she should be in a huge spa bath full of pink champagne followed by the beautician and hairdressers bit and finally all the bridesmaids dressing and pampering her. I was really thinking of me I guess and maybe wishing it was, NAH! No time for that.

So here I was in the place all alone suddenly. In the first moments I just looked around the empty hall with boxes and shit all over the tables and there was no possible way that I could feel alone. Not with the known fact that this room would in two short hours be full of people. I'd best get my finger out and do something with this hall and make it look like a wedding was happening. Far ou,t I had a lot to do but I did still had most of a bottle of champers and the rest of the bar if necessary.

Right then! Into it Naughty Nickers. What first?

Tables, ok then we need—no ah maybe the balloons. Start again Nick. Table cloths first, ok, then napkins, ashtrays, a few nibbles. No, too early for that. Go on to the decorations next. The main table is what we need set up first, the table for the lucky couple. So I started on that with the streamers in matching colours to the bridal group. I had also found the best lace table cloths for these four tables and once I had the main table finished, I felt like I was finally getting somewhere and the rest seemed to come together easily. All in all. it didn't look half-bad if I do say so myself.

A few people popped in during this time that I was preparing the place, to drop off stuff (food) but no one seem to wanna help out. Oh well. Then a few kids came in and they were great. Anything I wanted done, they buttered bread, blew up the balloons; a job I was not looking forward to, and last of all helped themselves to a few of the goodies. Kids, don't ya love 'em.

At about ten to three I rushed into the loo, ripped off me clobber and put on the beautiful blue dress that Hippy Lee had bought for this occasion. For the first time in a long time I was actually slim and lookin' good. I slapped on a bit of make-up and bolted across the road just in time to witness the wedding vows. It was a shame I was the last one there because I could hardly hear any of the celebrant's words. It didn't really matter much though because I knew the pair of them would say **I DO, I WILL, ALWAYS**.

I'm so happy for Pammy. She's thee person in the entire world who deserves happiness. She's always been the biggest giver, with the biggest heart. Pam has helped everyone who has ever crossed her path in some way or another. There was always some lost soul living on her lounge, me included. It was one of my happiest days in a long time.

Probably because I've never been married and by the looks of things, I never will be.

Back at the reception the Band played and everyone danced and partied as they would. A few of Pam's relos commented on how gorgeous I looked, the best I'd ever looked apparently. I owed it to Hippy Lee I s'pose, because he made me care about my appearance because he was always telling me how beautiful I was and that I should use it.

About half way through the night, one of the female guests asked her all time mate and the father of her three kids, "When are you going to marry me baby?" The male in question turned round and said, "You're too much of a bitch and I'll never marry you." At that she got rather nasty and proceeded to hurl plate after plate across the room at him.

It was sort of a hit and miss project. The older set, at the wedding, had just spent the past hour and a half washing, drying and stacking all these plates and here's this bitch smashing them one after another at her intended—or never intended—as the case may be. Well, do you think her bloke was gonna take this lightly. Huh! He grabbed the fire hydrant hose and let loose. Chicky-Babe was slammed up against the kitchen wall with a Ka-splat and there she was pinned to the wall until he started to enjoy his power. Then he went on to the next innocent victim and the next flattening each one to the wall. Unfortunately one of the victims was the blushing bride herself.

Because I'd been through enough violence very recently, I turned into a nervous wreck and decided it was time to go. I ended up with a couple of passengers for the way home and dropped them all home, round this way and that, left and right no problems. I was definitely over the limit but I felt I was ok to drive. (as usual) After dropping them off I was going up a road, well known to me and back to Pam's and I hit a keep left sign on the right hand side of the car. Oh shit! Water pissed out everywhere, the keep left sign was flattened to the ground and I was drunk. Woooops! I shoved the car across the road a bit and into the side street and went to sleep.

I'm not sure how much later it was, but I woke up to the sound of drunken singing and wondered where I was. I pieced it all together fairly quickly and realized these were all the young lads from the Wedding, staggering home.

Half the party goers were from the Islands, so a good percentage of them were staying at Pam's on the mainland. I'd rather be there. I had a quick piss and staggered in the direction of the noise, caught up with the young fellas at the cross-roads and continued on. I really wanted a drink because I had the dry horrors by then. Wayne passed me the cask bladder to have a drink. Yuk! No way I can do that to myself. "It's not wine Nick, It's scotch and cola." Says Wayne. Naturally I didn't believe him. "Oh well, don't have any then," he says, and has another huge scull out of the tap. Mmmm I'll give it a go. So we shared that on our walk back to Pam's which was about 3 km from there. I was mighty glad to be back there too. The lights were all out and it was time for bed. I found my allotted lounge, which was still vacant, and crashed.

Morning came as it does, along with all the worries and woes of the now broken car. Oh shi,t how am I going to get my silly self back home. Then after that I realized as well that I'd lost the hundred bucks that I had down my stockings.

Pam got up and was pleased to see that I had survived the night. Then she told me the rest of her story for "**THE WEDDING NIGHT FROM HELL**", she called it.

After I left, Woody, the bloke with the hose, continued on with his antics. By now he'd soaked most of the wedding party, including some of the more civilized guests and of course Pam, herself. She told me a lot of people left just after I did and then Ray disappeared as well. She decided to go home with J.B.s mother and get into some dry clothes.

On her way home she got pulled up by Mr. Plodd. He wanted to fine Pam for defects on the car and one light out at the back. Pammy just cried, "Some wedding day this has turned out to be." The cop then wanted to know why they were soaking wet too and she explained that part and also that her new Husband was missing in action. After some thought, Mr. Plodd said if she had some proof that it really was her Wedding Day he would let her off. Pam produced an also dripping wet wedding certificate and he let them go. That was the only one good thing that happened in the latter part of the evening, for Pam anyway. After getting dry clothes on she went back to the reception room and started cleaning the place. The colours from the wet streamers had run everywhere and had stained the tiles in the kitchen and most of the floor. There were smashed plates as well to be cleaned up and she had to collect all her own gear to take home again. It's a pity I had fucked off and fucked up because I could have helped her, but I was asleep in my broken car while all this was going on.

Apparently the hall had to be all cleaned up by 9am for a Church meeting so Pam had to have it all done and spent her wedding night, till nearly 4 in the morning to do this all on her own. What a distasteful ending to an objectionable evening. Poor Pam. At least she got through the wedding vows before everything went haywire, and she finally found her husband as well.

Next thing was to organize my car or at least get it back to Pam's. Ray and J.B. said they'd go down and get the car and drive it back or tow it, whatever the case may be. J.B. did drive it back but the water pissed out the radiator all the way and it was obvious I wasn't getting home with it like that. I rang all over the place to try and find an auto radiator for a HZ and there were none anywhere in Brisbane; so another problem to face.

After remembering about the 100 bucks again—Pam suggested we go back to where the car was and search the area, so we did that. Much to my surprise, after about half an hour of searching, Pam found the 2 fifties wrapped together and floating downstream in my piss. God we laughed our heads off then. That made the whole scenario a lot more amusing to us and to everyone that Pam told for the rest of the day.

I still had the serious shit to deal with, which was getting home to the kids. Ray decided that the only way left was to repair the existing radiator. Araldite! We got the radiator out and drained and dried it then bogged it up everywhere with an extra large tube. Waited the appropriate few hours and whacked it back in. We then had to jack the car body away from the fan, and shoved a lump of wood in there to use as a wedge.

I set off on the 300km drive back home carrying heaps of excess water. I got three quarters of the way home and it was boiling its guts up and I had no choice but to stop. At least I was over the Black Butt Range I thought to myself. I rang the friend that had the kids and told her of all that had happened. She was cool. Then I rang Pam and informed her I was getting there and I would make it home and then I went for a well deserved beer or two to let the car have time to cool down.

Another hour later and I was home with the kids. I was so glad to finally get home that night. I was also lucky that our little bodge job held out all this way. Glad to be home but once again a nervous wreck to be back here and so close to Hippy Lee again.

After a few days Lee showed up and started yelling and screaming from his car, "You've got my best piece, you fucking bitch. I want it back and I want it now."

Karen and Heath pulled up and tried to calm him down but he just got more irate and started yelling at Karen and salivating at the mouth and jumping up and down. I was reduced to a quivering mess once again and didn't know what he was going on about. Heath finally managed to calm him down to some degree and got him to leave the property. Apparently what he was after was some lingerie item that I still had. I thought he'd bought all this nice stuff for me, wrong, now he wants it all back.

Heath insisted I go to the cops with him right then and there and put in a protection order. I really did not want to do this—I never put a protection order on Jarmas or Mat-Mat why start now. What's the good of a piece of paper if someone wants to kill you? I've always believed that this would just make matters worse and that the already agro bloke will be even more pissed off when served with a protection order. It wasn't the case though and everything calmed down and Lee never came up to the cul-de-sac in the middle of the night again.

The next few weeks were totally uneventful and I was bloody glad of that. I got most of the inside of the house painted and a few more jobs done off the long list from the council. Then a bit later as I got back to my old self, I decided to have a painting party to get all the outside done, just as I had done on Macleay.

I had bugger all money as usual, so I bought 40 litres of shed paint, mission brown, for $42.00 and this was enough to cover the whole house. God it looked lovely. (sarcasm) The following week I went round all the trim with an apricot colour and it didn't look too bad then.

Who really cares anyway as long as it gets the council pass.

Time was running out with them and I still had the stumps to tie down, a few windows to put in and I still needed another water tank to make up the 5000 gallons that all residents had to have.

As it happened, a girlfriend of mine on the Island gave me a 2000 gal water tank for my Birthday, because the Islands had since gone on to mainland water. Wonderful, Lisa darling, all I had to do was get it from Macleay and then the next 300 kms back up here again. Interesting concept. Whatever the case it must be accomplished, because I needed water and I needed to get this house finalized so Dad could get his 12 grand back. It was his life insurance and if anything happened in the meantime I'd never forgive myself.

Me ol' mate Jimery (Pam's brother) said he'd help me with the whole project and help build me a tank stand as well. I naturally had to take him up on his offer because there was no other way I was gonna manage all that on my own. Jimery was a lot of fun as well and I felt I needed a bit of fun.

I traveled down to Brissy with Stu' and Ebony for the first part of the mission, which was to get the tank off the Island and up to Pam's place. Unfortunately I had no tow bar so even this small mission needed a borrowed car.

Another mate on the Island borrowed his brother's car and trailer and was leaving them at the Mainland jetty near the barge. We had lined up to borrow Lisa's Dad's truck to get the tank from her house

3km to the Island jetty and we had a couple of helpers to get it off the truck and rolled up on to the barge. No worries mate!

No worries at all until there was a loud knocking on Lisa's back door at 5am and there's a very stressed looking Cris. "My brother's car and trailer have been stolen from the Jetty during the night and he's absolutely rope-able. He'll probably never speak to me again."

Oh shit, oh no. I thought it was called Murphy's Law. If anything can go wrong it will. I'm thinking I should change it to Nicky's Law. I felt so terrible for him and for his brother. What could I say. Cris was pissed off and then he just pissed off. I didn't even know whether he had insurance or not. Lisa, Jimery and I sat round working out a new plan. Naturally Pam would have to be involved because she was on the Mainland and we weren't. We finally came up with a new plan but it just meant I had to go home again and come back down at a later date. Which means more dollars, but there was no choice. We got the tank off the Island and up to Pam's that day with her car and an unregistered box trailer.

Then home again I went without a tank which just set me back a bit more time on this bloody council final. I went back to Brisbane the following weekend in the Just-Holdin'-Together and my dearest mate Pam had organized yet another trailer which I could hang on to for a week or two before having to return it.

I planned to leave at about 4am the next morning when there's no traffic on the road. I always have preferred driving in the wee hours of the morning, it's so much less drama specially with a fucking great tank on the back. When I got there Jimery was dressed to kill and ready to take me out for the night. "I have no dollars Jim, only enough to get home again."

"Don't worry Nick, just go get changed and let's go."

"What the hell, if you're shouting me." I told you Jim was fun, and I might as well start having some. We went to the Grand Hotel at Cleveland this time and had a great time there. After that we went back to his old mate's place just round the corner. At some point in time, Pat, the mate got a bit touchy, feely and was touching my hands on the table. Jim lost the plot and started yelling at his ol' mate. "Keep your fucking hands to yourself—keep your hands off my woman."

Don't know where he got the 'My Woman' bit from. I guess he must just go along with every male in existence. If you've spoken to them for any length of time or if they bought you a drink, or if you went so far as to fuck them, then consider yourself a possession from there on in.

I said, "I'm big enough and ugly enough to look after myself Jimery, so shut your mouth. He promptly left in my car at a great rate of knots and I was left with his mate and the wife and five kids. Didn't bother me too much because I still felt like another few scotches and Pat said he'd call me a cab later. His wife worked for Yellow Cabs. Ha!

I got home to Pam's about midnight and Jim was not home yet and my car was not back either. Not much I can do about it now, so I went straight to bed in my usual spot and passed out immediately.

I woke just before 4am because Pam had the alarm on for me and Jim, so we could leave by 4.30 after a cuppa. I went straight outside and to my surprise the trailer complete with tank was attached to my particular vehicle and ready to go. Good shit. I grabbed my bits and pieces from the house and got ready to leave. I tried to start the car. Nothing. I tried again and again. Nothing. I sat there for a few minutes thinking about it and working myself to boiling point. It went yesterday. Everything was fine yesterday. What's wrong now that wasn't wrong yesterday. Why won't it go. I jumped out of the car swearing, "Fuck you Jimery," slammed the door. "Fuck you for this." Opened the bonnet, looked into the pitch black space and then slammed the fucker again. He'd done something to stop me going without him, I just knew it.

I stomped back into the house and put the kettle back on. Of course Pam had heard the calamity and was just coming down the stairs. She told me over a coffee that Jim had come in very late and he was crazy mad. He'd even broken a stubby over his own stupid head.

She didn't know where he went and all she did know was that he brought the car back and got it ready to go.

"He's done something to it, Pam. He's pulled something out or off it and it won't go. He's not gonna let me go without him the possessive bastard. It's my car, my house, and my fucking tank."

At that moment in staggered Jimery, hair everywhere (what's left of it). He had been asleep on the trampoline until it did flip flops on him and he ended up under it. Obviously he was asleep on the very edge and it flipped over and landed on top of him and that's where he stayed.

"I still wanna take you and your tank home Nick. Please forgive me. Please Nick you need me. Don't do it alone"

"How the fuck can I—you've taken some shit out of my car and it's not going any-fucken-where any-fucken-way and I don't know why. I'm just a stupid fucking female anyway, Hey Jim-er-y!" For a person who normally had a lot to say he kept his mouth shut and disappeared again.

Pam explained. "He's just so embarrassed Nick because he's lost his teeth and he still wants to take you home and help build the stand but he can't go without his teeth. I got over my dark mood almost immediately and was overcome with a huge desire to laugh my head off. Which we both did for a time. Ha Ha Ha, the sharp dressed man lost his teeth. When we got over our laughter we got back to the project and started to retrace the moves that young Jimery may have staggered.

I went back to my own thoughts and to the tank and the car. He must've been in the car and under the bonnet and round the trailer because he did all that last night. We started on a new search and with a little team effort, hey presto, we finally found them in a pile of spew in the back seat of the HZ. He who laughs last laughs the loudest.

Pam gave them back to Jim and pretended I knew nothing. She also explained that he'd best clean up the spew and get the car going real quick, before I burst a blood vessel. In fact I was trying not to burst at the seams laughing. I'm laughing now. By the time I'd had one more cup of coffee for the road, Jimery had recovered his decorum (and teeth). It's a shame it was rush hour by now, but Jim was driving and told me not to stress.

It was a long haul and with a few scary moments where we got the wobbles up a bit. At one stage going over the Black Butt Ranges I thought we would just blow away. The look on Jim's face told me he wasn't without fear either.

At Nanango Town we bought a well deserved carton and went to ol' mate Karen's place to celebrate finally getting home—Sweet Home Nanango! Karen had a major hangover and told us later that she had thought it was a 747 about to crash land on her roof. She was more than pleased to see us pair of idiots with a tank and a carton as well. We had a couple of beers there but alas we still had one more leg of the journey to go.

It was so good to get to the old dump and I was genuinely glad and happy to be home. We weren't here but five minutes and Jim slapped a blue sheet of paper on the dining room table and said, "If you sign this Nicky, we could be married in a month." I laughed at him and flicked my hand just past his earhole and said, "Don't be soooo ridiculous Jimery, there's a carton in the fridge," and with that off I went to get a coldie. He didn't drop the subject immediately but in the end he gave me the paper to put away and I could sign it whenever I was ready. We'll see. Maybe I would never be ready. Maybe I'd never be ready for him or anyone else ever again.

Jimery was a trier though, he ran himself ragged over the next few days doing all sorts of jobs that needed doing. He dug and he shoveled, he hammered and nailed. He even collected rocks from all round the circular driveway and made a big love heart with Jimery loves Nicky in the middle. This sort of sickened me a bit. I'm not the romantic I used to be, I guess. Love doesn't seem so important any more. It never got me anywhere only into more trouble and more pain.

Life was good just how it was, why confuse things. "I really have had more than enough relationships Jim, you're a great friend and I want it to stay that way."

He was very patient with me because he knew all about Hippy Lee and what had gone on, not so long ago.

As it happened Lee ended up back in the picture once more. It was my fault of course, isn't it always. I went round to see him didn't I?. I know I shouldn't have, but circumstances led me back there. I'd been in Nanango at a Funeral. It was terrible, but then funerals generally are. This one was exceedingly worse though because it had been a suicide. How terrible one must feel, to take their own life. To think, I almost did that myself. I was lucky I got back up the stairs that night or I wouldn't be writing this bloody book.

At the funeral the kids said their poems for their Mother and various speeches were made, then we all went to the pub afterwards for the wake. I stayed for a couple and then I stood and said, "Di would want us all to drink and be happy because she's out of her pain now." Then I left and drove silently home. I kept the 2 flowers which were to throw on the grave, one for me and one for Lee. All the way home I tossed around in my head whether to go and see him or not. He had apparently made quite a few attempts on his life since we had split.

Well the bloody car seemed to turn down his street instead of going straight ahead and home to Jim and my kids. Silly car. Huge mistake. Lee's sister said he was home and directed me out to the back patio where the very desolate looking Lee sat drinking a quite scotch.

"Hello Nicky," he said in an uninterested tone. "Hi Lee, I've just come to give you a flower and a message to go with it. I've kept one for you and one for myself—No matter how bad things seem it's not worth ending your life over. I explained to him where I'd been and why and then I burst into tears.

"Please Lee, please, please promise you won't try to kill yourself again. I couldn't stand it. I still care about you. I just couldn't stand it if you were dead and it's my fault." He seemed to change his tune and said, "Can we at least be friends now?"

"Yes I'd love that if we could be friends." I stayed a little while and we just chatted about general stuff and then I said my goodbyes and went home.

I went home as usual to my own home and my own bed. *Single Bed, Single Bed, there ain't no room for your sweet head.*

Jim had done dinner and I was wrapped about that, but he made a big deal about me going to see Lee. I told him the whole truth and nothing but the truth, but he didn't believe me. You can always tell. He had no right anyway. I was upset and went to see a friend, that's all. He was still pretty pissed about it though.

I just wanted him to be my mate, my best friend but in my experience you can't be too close to a male and then the Best friend bit goes out the door. Geffory was probably right to feel the way he did, because he loved me and wanted me to marry him, other than that he was right. Two days later Hippy Lee turned up with a bottle. He'd come around to meet the new boarder. Naturally Jim didn't like the boarder bit and started playing up. Lee, as we know is a player, and so he played Mr. Cool as a cucumber as he walked casually through to the dining area and sat down.

This must be the part where I get to say—"You could cut the air with a knife". Fucked if I would have expected it but next minute the two of them are sharing piss and pot and nothing else mattered. (Least of all the owner of the house) They both spent the rest of the night out-doing each other on every aspect of husbandry. It was really quite disgusting. I just got drunk, it was the best thing I could think of at the time. Then I went to bed and they would maybe have noticed. Who would know.

Oh at least everything's cool, Nick. It's gonna be OK, Lee just wants to be friends. Every one needs good friends, don't they?

When I woke up I laid there and thought about it all for awhile and realized I was in the shit again. Lee had been saying how much he loved me and that means trouble. The bloke was always perfectly fine unless his emotions got involved. He really was a multi personality. The bloke I fell in love with was the hippy and then there was the vicious bastard who cared for nothing and no one, the female, (she was OK as long as she had her own lingerie), the intellect and Mr.

Fantasy, who lived in a world with all the characters from the Never Ending Story. I can pick 'em.

In entered Jim with a coffee for me, what a love. He looked out the window and said, "Hey, who's this in a red Datsun. I think it's Lee. I sat bolt up in bed and leaned over as far as I could to look out the window. Yes it definitely was him—here he was, first thing in the morning. And for what? Oh fuck, I'll go out Jimery, you stay here. I can talk to him better than if you come out as well.

SEEMS I WAS WRONG

Lee came through the front door as I got to the lounge doorway yielding a mattock or a pick axe. (not funny Nick) He flashed past me and up the hallway after Jim. Jim wasn't far behind me and ran up the hallway and leapt out the back door (still no stairs) and bolted.

Actually, like I told the court at a later date, "I'm really not sure exactly what happened but I know he beat the fuck out of me." I was in my bedroom by then watching Lee smash the mattock through the back window after Jim had long gone and run down the block somewhere. As usual it was my problem. Where are the kids? Ka bang, ka bang, ka bang, crunch, ughhhhh! I can't describe the sound of a fanny being kicked in by steel cap boots, I'm sorry but this is the best I can do.

I was in the bedroom on the floor for—some length of time, but I had to get up. I had to find the kids. They've always been cleverer than I give them credit for and fortunately they kept out of sight. I managed to stagger to the lounge and then fell over into the first chair there. It was right opposite the front door. I sat there in a state of shock, just staring out the front door. Lee came back a second time. I was looking straight at him and yet I did not see him. SMACK. He hit me in the earhole this time with the flat of an axe. I could still see his lips moving too but I could only guess that he was still screaming at me. His mouth was still moving—I know that much.

I know this sounds really whimpish but I just closed my eyes then and waited for the next whack. I still had my eyes scrunched tightly shut when I heard the car pull out of the driveway. Then I fell to pieces, tiny little pieces. Then the kids came from their hiding spots and to my side. "Are you all right Mum? Mum are you all right?" I felt so weak I could hardly answer. I can't remember this bit much but I know they were there because they weren't anywhere else. Then we heard a car coming back. Oh no we've gotta get out of here. It was Jim though and I couldn't move anyway. There was blood dripping off my ear and I could NOT move.

Jimery came in. "Oh no, Nick are you all right?" Apparently not. A few more moments and the Police arrive. Oh my God no. I can't face this. They wanted answers to all their stupid questions and all I could do was look at the very interesting pattern on the carpet. (it's plain) The Plodd or the police could see they were not gonna get anything out of me at this point in time, so they just told me to go see a doctor and report to them after that. Mmmmmmm.

I think I stayed in that same chair for the next day or so. Jim looked after me though, made cups of tea and coffee all day, looked after the kids. Made dinner for us all night after night. He was a real good friend.

I recovered as always I have. Snap out of it Nicky, just snap out of it. Within the next few weeks, Jim was hassling me again. "You'd love a fucking tall, ugly bastard that hits you but you can't love me. You just can't love me."

"I can't love any one any fucking more Jimery. Fuck you, Fuck the whole boiling lot of you." I'm screaming this two inches from his face.

I was going out to the car with Ebony in my arms and telling Stuart to get in the car too. The Volvo. While I was getting Stuart, who'd just woken up, Jim took the fucking guts out of the ignition AGAIN! Should have realized the first time hey, you say. Should have—but did not.

SHIT! SHIT! SHIT! Now I'll have to stay here and listen to his shit or ring someone else to come and get me out of here. I rang Mr. Hate, a fellow who I'd been cleaning for, for a short time. He was a nice quite, mild mannered fellow and he came and got me and the kids, no worries mate. We all stayed at Mr. Hate's place for the night. He only lived about 4kms from my place.

When Mr. Hate took me home in the morning, Jim had left taking the Volvo with him but before doing so he managed to trash my house. He'd put his head through dining room wall before I left with Mr. Hate but now he had also tipped a whole kilo bag of plaster all over the place and wet it as well.

Thanks for your time and you can thank me for mine, and after that's said, forget it.

CHAPPIE 15

MR. HATE (MY FRIEND)

Once again I was left without a car, but why the fuck should I possess a car when the Jimerys and the Jamas of the world don't have one. How dare I be better off than they are? At that rate why should I have a house either? I'm sure this is the reasoning in their tiny minds for why they smash holes in my house or my head.

After Mr. Hate had seen the plaster everywhere and the missing car, I guess he felt sorry for me. He offered to pick me up on payday and take me shopping. I took him up on this offer as I had no other choice. Next I had to find out where my car was or where Jim had gone in it, which wasn't terribly hard, because he went straight back to Pam's.

Pam was living back on Lamb Island again and Jim had gone there and taken my car to my Dad's place, on Macleay. My next mission was to get my arse down there and get it back again—great! It still wasn't registered either and now I had no Keys because Jim through them in the bush. Mr. Hate said he could drive me down the Island the following weekend. I was lucky to have someone to help me out at a time like this. I knew why though, there's always got to be some reason and no one does nothing for nothing.

Unfortunately on the first night I went round to Mr. Hates, I was pretty pissy and pretty pissed off as well, with Jim and Lee and probably my whole fucking life. I got more pissed at Mr. Hate's place as well and I crossed the dreaded line. You know the one—where friends are friends and lovers are lovers and never the twain shall meet. Well I was his cleaner and his friend and it should have remained that way but the drunken Nicky is really like another person. A person who's got no idea what she's doing or why, sometimes. If only the sober Nicky could stop her, but she is so much stronger and she'll do whatever the hell she likes, when she likes. There's no stopping her at all when she's on a mission. So now I'd given another of my good friends a taste of the forbidden fruit and now he wanted more. Of course he would, what did I expect, after all he is a male.

Mr. Hate did take me down to Brisbane and I went over the Island to get my Volvo. I had no problems starting the car but when I was driving down the Island to the barge the steering lock came into action and I had to shove a butter knife into it to keep it free. While on the barge I jammed the knife in to the lock part and taped it up round the steering column. I hoped this would do till I got home.

When I got to the mainland I was re-checking all this shit when Mat-Mat showed up. Oh great! He can probably break the lock altogether, I hoped. He had a largie in his paw too—what's new. I helped him drink it while he was stuffing around with the car. Then we sat chatting for awhile and I helped him drink another one. Mr. Hate pulled up then to make sure I'd got my car all right and he said he'd go and get Stuart (who'd stayed at a mate's) and then follow me up the highway towards Nanango. "OK Mr. Hate, thanks a lot for your help. I'll see you back up there then." Off he went. Mat then caught the next boat home to the Island, after failing to break the steering lock, and I headed on the long road home.

The car did a slight detour at the Redland Bay Hotel and the Naughty Nicky ordered 2 largies of Strongbow for the trek. I had no more dramas with the steering lock and we were cruising merrily along. I had Ebony with me as well and we stopped off for sandwiches somewhere and then continued on. Just before Esk, I ran out of petrol. It was about 5kms out actually. I couldn't believe it. What a stupid bitch, fancy running out of petrol. Shortly after some nice fella stopped and asked if I wanted help. "Oh I'm such an idiot, I've run out of petrol. I'm not used to the car you see and just didn't realize that on the E in this particular car, it stopped dead, and was completely empty. I gave the bloke $10.00 and an empty can and hoped to Christ he would return.

While waiting, I decided to roll a large joint out of one of the 2 ounces I had, had another slurp of Strongbow and sat there looking at the glorious view. I was situated halfway up a steep hill looking across the mountains of Esk and the surrounding area. There I was waiting for my petrol when in the rear vision I spot Mr. Plodd pull up behind me. Oh Shit! Oh serious amounts of shit. I hurl the bottle in front of the still sleeping Ebony; ditched the joint and stuffed half of Ebony's sandwich in my gob while leaping out of the car to acknowledge Mr. Plodd.

With my mouth still chomping and over full, I managed to garble out, "some bloke is coming back with petrol any minute. Thanks anyway." Suddenly it started to piss down, I mean like cats and dogs. He gave me a slight wave still just getting out of his own car, got back in and did a U-eee over the double whites and he was gone. My heart was still almost in my mouth along with the remains of the sandwich and still I did manage to breathe a sigh of relief. The trustworthy bloke came back with the tin of petrol and I was once again on the road. Ebony slept on.

Mr. Hate was already at my place when I got there, God knows when he passed me, probably while I was stopped in the pissing rain, who knows. At least he was there with my Stuey Bluey and I was more than thankful to get home on this particular occasion. Why do I do these things, I have to ask myself. I really don't have any answers. It seems to be a mixture between alcoholism and the connection with the criminal element that I've so often crossed paths with over the past 10 years.

Mr. Hate wasn't like that, he was a good man. A mild mannered and gentle sort of man. Not my cup of tea really. Not that I can figure out why I keep going for the big, huge, rough, tough types, because I always wanted them to change, to be more gentle and more caring and to be less criminalistic. It was mainly Jarmas I wanted to calm down a bit, but that was so long ago now. I had wished he was more like Mr. Hate and now I find myself wishing Mr. Hate was more like him. Jarmas is the one trapped inside my heart and I can't seem to get rid of him no matter how many years go by.

As fate would have it I found myself pregnant again after 6 years, Unbelievable. I had decided after Ebony, I would never have any more children, well not unless it was to Jarmas anyway. I really didn't want to have 2 children to 2 different Fathers. I've never been happy about that fact and here I was pregnant to a 3rd different father—namely Mr. Hate. Oh Christ, we weren't even in a relationship. I did not want any more relationships either and here I was pregnant. Can you have one without the other? Here I was trim taught and terrific for the first time in a long time too, still I did always want a large family; oh what a dilemma. A month of so went by and here I was with that choice and a huge decision to make. I really did want another baby. I would have had at least 6 given the right circumstances. Finally I told Mr. Hate of my dilemma and he said, "Well it is your choice Nicky." Great, leave it all up to me. No offer of love or marriage, just "Oh well it's your choice." Bloody typical of a male. He didn't seem to have a problem with choosing whether to fuck me or not while I was blind drunk, did he. No problem at all. I felt used, but what is new. I've always been used and abused, when the going gets tough the tough get going, going, gone. Maybe it's all I deserve.

Another month went by and time was running out. A decision had to be made right now. On the way into town with Mr. Hate one day, I simply said, "I'm not going down to Tweed Heads."

Mr. Hate ever-so lightly rested his hand on my knee and replied, "Oh I am pleased."

No excitement, no thrill in his voice, no sudden pulling up of the car to shower me with love and kisses, nothing. In fact I'm sure I could have told him I'd just passed my driving test and got the same thrilling result. He was so undemonstrative. But! I had made my decision, my choice and that's that. On the way home again, I told him that I wasn't sure of an on going relationship at all and that I'd just decided I wanted the baby. His answer was "If ever you're not happy, just say so and I'll leave." Sounds simple enough, doesn't it.

It was round this time that Mr. Jarmas arrived just to confuse the issue. He came at about 4am and just cruised into my bedroom through the french doors and woke me up. I thought I was dreaming or at least having a nightmare. There he was just looking down at me from next to my bed with a largie in his hand (VB of course). Far out! I couldn't believe my eyes. I rubbed the sleep out of them and had another look. Yes it was definitely him, after all these years. Nearly 4 years of nothing and now here he is standing in my bedroom at 4am no less. I still loved him. I knew straight away. God only knows why, after all he'd done to me and that he had not done for his daughter. No way in the world was I gonna let him know that though.

I got up and had a few beers with him and we chatted for a couple of hours. I got to ask all the unanswered questions that had been in the back of my mind for all these years. It didn't help any but I got to ask. Jarmas wanted to wake Ebony up then and I said, "Yes I s'pose you can—after all she is your daughter." I think once he had woken her up and took one look at her for the first time in all these years, he did, finally, believe that she was.

Jarmas was nervous and twitchy and obviously freaking out about something. He kept saying I can't stay long, I'll have to get going soon. He was on the run maybe or on speed or something. Then he wanted to take Ebby into town and buy her something nice. I wouldn't let him take her alone so we all ended up going to town. Had a really nice day together. When we came home he did a bit of work on Ebby's bike and then he fixed Stuart's as well. He always was good with the kids. Both kids. There was no favoritism.

He had arrived in a XC Station Wagon and told me he couldn't leave in it because it was hot and that he had got it for me to replace my $8 000 worth of Transit Van. Some people never learn. I'm one of them. Stupid, Stupid me let him take my Volvo in the end. I told him I did not want this hot car, not ever and he'd have to come back and get rid of it. He said he could do a deal and swap my Volvo for another Van or another station wagon that was clean and that he'd bring that back to me and take the XC away.

When he was actually going I asked him to please take me round to Mr. Hate's on his way out. I didn't want him to think I was doing nothing and going nowhere. Then he sat round at Mr. Hate's for the next 4 or 5 hrs. I still believe to this day that he was waiting for me to say, "I love you Jarmas, please stay. Of course I could not say those words. I couldn't let myself and he finally left.

His coming like that made it harder still, for me to get on with my life and to get on with a new relationship with Mr. Hate. I sort of kept my distance to a point, I had a boarder at my place too, named Paul. He was there mainly to help with finances but his presence made the situation easy to handle. Mr. Hate continued to live at his place and me at mine. I could not commit, not to anyone.

Time drifted slowly on and the next amusing event was Jarmas' head on TV. Ebony yelled out to me, "Mummy, Daddy's on the Tely." That could only mean one thing. Trouble with a capital T. Yes it was him, and yes he was in the shit again. "Mind your head sir," was what the cop was saying to a hand-cuffed unhappy looking Jarmas and there in the background was my Volvo. Again this man had got me for a car.

Here we go again, now I was car-less and would have to get something else quickly or, rely totally on Mr. Hate. Well the latter would never do, so I definitely have to buy another. I most certainly wasn't touching the hot one which was still sitting there, on my property. As it happened my sister had an old Corolla which still had a few weeks rego on it and she was gonna sell it to the wreckers, but decided I could have it. So down to Brisbane I go again and bring that back up here. It went pretty well just looked really shitty, oh well.

About two weeks later I rolled it on one of these really bad dirt roads on a sharp bend. Paul and I had gone out to Wooroolin Pub to get some supplies for a party at a mate's place. We did go in for one drink and I mean ONE, I had a Bloody Mary, in fact and then we left. I was only doing about 60km but the corner was sharper than I expected and we started to fish tail all over the place and then up a bit of a bank and over and then over again back on it's feet. Shit. What's happening. The three of us were all white and there were clouds of white dust throughout the car. What is this? "Are we allright?"

"Are you all right Ebony?"

We had all survived unscathed and I thought the next best thing to do was leap out—just in case of petrol leaking. The clouds of white all over us and all through the car was a zip top pack of washing powder that did the roll over with us. This became a great source of amusement after we realized we were all OK. I have a huge mop of curly hair and so had Paul and we were just covered in the stuff and initially thought p'raps we were in heaven, no such luck. We all got out and checked out the damage, the car was a complete write off. It had a flat tyre on the driver front, the windscreen was smashed and the main body looked like it had been through the wringer. Another amusing point was that all six largies were still intact including the ones on the road and so was the green ginger wine, Unbelievable.

After a few minutes of collecting our valuables, and ourselves, I tried the car. It started. I thought I might as well limp home in it, because it couldn't do any harm. Paul had rolled a large joint and I had opened the bottle of Green Ginger Wine. So picture this, a dark blue shitty Corolla with three people in it covered in soap powder. Paul with a Bob Marley style joint, hanging out of his gob and his feet crossed and out the windscreen resting on the bonnet and me slurping on a bottle of Green Ginger, travelling at 5km an hour. (Medicinal purposes of course) Imagine if the Plodd came by now. We laughed.

About 2kms up the track some nice people pulled up and insisted on taking us home and leaving the wreck where it was. We agreed. They took us back to the designated barbie and we thought we'd go back and get the car when Mr. Hate and the other fella got home from work. When Mr. Hate did get there I didn't notice immediately and Ebony ran out and said, "Mummy just rolled the car." The poor bastard probably thought I was dead, or had lost the baby. He breathed a sigh of relief when he realized neither was the case and everyone was fine.

We did go back and get the wreck, but it was a waste of time really and I was car-less once again. Mr. Hate reckoned the front end on it was stuffed and that, plus the freshly graded road and sharp bend had all been contributing factors to our flipping it. Never a dull moment!

As I've said before, I'm sure—life went on and I got **fatter** and **fatter** and **fatter.** Mr. Hate loved the fat because it was him that put it there. This protruding belly was not mine but his. He came round nearly every day and if he didn't I usually went round there. The company was always good and as for love, who knows? Apparently it can grow. I think not.

As I only have 2 tanks and they were both empty, I was convinced it would be a good idea for me to now move to his house where he could look after me. He didn't really want the children there as well but it's a package deal. Me and 2 kids. Don't look a gift horse in the mouth Nicky, and I didn't because it's really hard to live without water.

So I moved myself, my kids and all our personal gear round to Mr. Hate's place. Stuart had to change school buses too, but that was OK, at least he didn't have to change schools.

It was OK staying there but once again my place, my home, was just sitting there empty, like when I was with Lozza. No concern what-so-ever for anything I had, or had done, just thinking completely and utterly of themselves. It was really nice to be driven around and looked after-ish and to know the bloke was home and would always come home, every day.

Mr. Hate was working at the TAFE at this point and I decided I needed a job as well to get some more money for the on-coming baby. I guess I didn't absolutely have to but because I had now moved in with Mr Hart, it cut down the usual pension I got, but didn't actually alter the costs I had.

I was round at Big Sal's place, and she was bitchin' about money too, and said we both need a job really Nick, these men aren't ever gonna provide for us the way we want. Which was more beer please. Then she told me of a peach picking job not too far away and we could share petrol costs.

"Well bloody ring up then."

"No you."

"No Problem." I rang and the pair of us presented ourselves to Mr. Patterson the following morning. He was more than impressed, this looks like a couple of hard workers he thought to himself. He was right of course and we both had jobs.

It kept me busy and kept my mind off the fact that Mr. Right had eluded me again, AND I was having a baby.

Me and big Sal had a ball really in those few months. She was great, a ball of laughs. She got the whole place laughing some days. It's a good thing we never laughed our heads off though, or we could'a fell off the ladder, dropped our joey pouch full of peaches and been sacked as well. She sang, she threw rotten peaches about, she loudly complained on a regular basis about the flies and about the heat and about anything at all you could possibly complain about.

Sally had a way to make the worst looking job seem fun. We both went through the thinning process and then had a couple of months off till it was time to do the fruit thinning and then finally the picking. By this time I was getting rather large and when Jeffery (The Boss) asked us if we'd be back for the next pick I replied "I'll probably be too fat to get up the ladder by then." He smirked and said, "I thought so Nicky, if you want to come back and just pick on all the bottoms of the trees, you're welcome. So it was agreed and I went back for 1 more session.

Finally I had to finish up at work, which was really my only freedom, but I was too fat and I was absolutely stuffed by the end of a day. Mr. Hate had me just where he wanted me, in his web. Another couple of months to go until the birth of my third child. God it's a long haul when it gets closer to the end—each day seems like an eternity.

Two months later.

Ebony was due to start grade one, Stuart was now in grade 7 and I was waiting, waiting, waiting. Ebony did not want to go to school at all and certainly not while I went off to have a baby. She didn't want to miss out and I didn't want her to miss her first day of school. We had major drama that morning. I had just had enough of being pregnant. I chased Ebony up the road in the car. Every time she stopped, I drove slowly up behind her and yelled, "Keep going, just keep going."

After half a dozen false alarms, Elliot finally came about 11 days late and we were all so pleased, especially me. He came on a Tuesday at about 9.30. The labour started about 4am and as soon as I tapped Mr. Hate, he leaped out of bed at an alarming rate and started dashing round like a chook with its head cut off. It was so funny to watch and I'd never seen anything like it before. I told him not to stress it was only mild at this stage but he couldn't get me in the car and into town fast enough. On the way in we were still picking out girl's names, because I had really already decided it would be a boy. So had Elliot been a girl she would have been named Tuesday.

Moments before Elliot arrived, the midwife told Mr. Hate to "go and have tea and toast, It will be awhile yet." At the second he walked back in was the crowning of the head and then out he came, a perfect little baby boy, *and his mumma cried.* Mr. Hate was cruising round with the video camera to get the first moments of life and the first bath on tape and I still had my legs widely spread in the stirrups waiting for the stitching session. It's really the worst moment of all. When they finally tell you, you can take your legs down now, and you can't actually move them.

Elliot was gorgeous and soooo tiny. One never remembers how tiny they are, especially not with a 6-year break in between. Mr. Hate was over the moon, he couldn't stop smiling and he hardly took his eyes off this little tiny boy. His little tiny boy.

After a few weeks back at Mr. Hate's home I thought I'd better go round to my place and check it out. Everything looked all right from the outside but once I got up the hallway I realized the arse end of the house was missing. It was smashed in by the water tank on the stand that Jim had built. Shit. Bloody Hell, my house was sitting empty and falling apart and here I was over at Mr. Hate's, cleaning and doing gardens etc. Sound familiar? Does to me. I wanted to go home, I had to go home. Things had to be sorted and insurance companies had to be contacted.

I never quite felt at home round Mr. Hate's place and I know the kids couldn't stand it. He was always on to them about opening the fridge or jumping on his shitty old life-line furniture or something. After all he didn't know children, or anything about them. He only knew his baby and would slowly learn all the other stuff as he watched Elliot grow.

I for one know how hard this can be because, if you remember in Chappy 3 the bloke had older kids and I knew nothing about them and only had the knowledge of my darling one yr old. I still reckon I made a good effort to be a part time mother.

Unfortunately I'm a bastard child and cannot be told, not anymore anyway. So now it was my turn and my trip and I'm the fucking BOSS! I remember one night when I got home late or latish, Mr. Hate refused to speak to me at all. HUH. That was the night before I left his place, actually. The silent treatment would never get ya anywhere, never got him anywhere at all. He refused to speak to me and refused to pass the joint. The super large joint that he had rolled. The same sort he had rolled for the past two years as a friend. But things were different now, though NICK, you're not just the drunk he took advantage of, you're now the mother of his baby and nothing more.

I came back home to my little removal shit box and reorganized the kids school buses again, etc. Initially Mr. Hate came round every day but went home at night and then after a time he mostly stayed here and went home sometimes. We were on a pension together now too, which basically means the bloke gets a bit more and the mother of the children (all three now) gets a bit less. I, of course was not impressed with this.

I knew Mr. Hate was not my perfect partner and I was not in love, but we had always been good friends and got on pretty well. As time went by he paid less and less attention to me and more and more to Elliot. It was great to finally see the Father of one of my kids give a dam, but he seemed to become obsessed and I was just the cook, house-keeper, and a bloody great fat one at that. I was unhappy, which meant Mr. Hate would have to go, as he had said he would. He did not go though, he just hung on and hung on and I went out more and more and drank more as well.

One morning when I was seriously hung over or still drunk, Mr. Hate left Elliot on the bed with me and poor Elliot fell off on his head. Oh Shit. I of course, blamed Mr. Hate for this and abused him loudly. He blamed me because I was the drunk, after all. After a bit of a screaming match (me doing all the screaming), I said "Why don't you fuck off and take your kid with you". Then I left and took my neighbor to town as planned.

By the time I got back, which was all of an hour, he had every last item of his packed, right down to the last teaspoon. He had his caravan hooked up and was almost ready to leave. I told him he could still go but he wasn't taking Elliot, but he continued on down the verandah. I grabbed his long ponytail to stop him and he twisted my hand backwards, breaking my thumb. Naturally I let go then with the pain and he left with Elliot. I sat on the top step and cried. It was so easy for him to leave once I had said "Take the kid with you". I never meant it at all, it was just there was no other way to get him to go and

I could not stand him anymore. I was running from my own home and from my own kids because he was there. It just built up more and more inside till this explosion. I was also drinking more, much more than usual.

I decided to leave well enough alone at this stage and went back into town to have my thumb checked and to cry on my best mate's shoulder. To drown my sorrows as well. My girlfriend said if I want him to leave and the relationship is over, then he must leave and go alone. I did feel sorry for Mr. Hate, but feeling sorry for someone is not a good enough reason to go on. It was just making me completely crazy.

The next morning first thing; I went round and called out, "You can't keep Elliot, Mr. Hate, you bring him outside and strap him in his seat or I'll call the police." Mr. Hate came out and strapped Elliot in the car. As he did so he said, I couldn't possibly look after him full time anyway, Nicky." He looked a pale shade of green. He looked like he would keel over and die. I still felt sorry for the poor old bloke but I just leapt in the car and took off again, it was the best way. I cried again and I felt terrible too, but it was different for me, I just did not love him, so I could not spend the rest of my life with him. Why go on and on if it just isn't right. It's hardest for the children too, and I reckon if the Daddy is gone early in the piece it doesn't affect the child quite as much.

Life went on as it does and Mr. Hate continued to visit on a regular basis and I mean regular, like every second day or so. I couldn't be nasty to him and I didn't want to be nasty, I just couldn't marry him. Then I met someone round the area who I quite fancied, but I didn't do anything about it because it just seemed wrong and I didn't wanna hurt Mr. Hate any more than I had done.

The next turn of events changed everything though. Mat showed up with his usual carton or two and so we got into that for awhile and then Mr. Hate showed up as he would and looked down his nose at me and whoever else was there. Because I never refused him access or a cuppa he just came in as normal and made a cuppa and made himself at home. After a while I just wanted to get out of there so I asked him to babysit (only Elliot) while me and an ol' mate went off on a piss mission into Nanango. I was so fucked up I didn't know what I wanted any more and happiness it seemed was not at the end of a bottle.

Mat-Mat drove into town. He was a bit pissy but I trusted his driving. We partied at the Fitz, for a few hours and were pretty well drunk by closing time. Mat had parked the car (my car) in the bottle shop drive through and when closing came, about seven of us, including my daughter, piled in the car with Mat once again at the wheel! Next thing the Plodd did a circle round the Pub and Mat got out. Everyone else stayed where they were. So guess which idiot got behind the wheel. Yep you guess it. Me. Christ how drunk and stupid can one person get. I took off out of there like a Bat out of Hell and headed out of town but the wrong way, and then I realized I've got nearly No petrol, so I turned down a side street. The cops were right behind me of course, and so then I pulled over and stopped. They reefed me out of the car and threw me onto the bonnet in the normal cop procedure. Their story about that was quite different, they said, I fell out of the car with a stubbie in my hand. Oh wel,l makes stuff all difference to the outcome.

By then Karen and Mat had arrived and she took Ebony with her and the Plodd carted me off to Kingaroy. They held me for ages, hassling me about who was the bloke standing by the car. I wouldn't tell naturally so they kept me and said, they'd go on all night. Finally the bitch cop found a tiny photo inside my wallet. It was a tiny piece of long ripped up photo, but you could definitely see who it was. "George R. Cl . . . ." she said. Then they finally said I could go. They even drove me back to Nanango, where I'd left my car. Not that I was allowed to drive it for 24 hours.

I couldn't believe how stupid I'd been. I was gonna lose my license for a start and if I didn't start thinking about it a bit I'd lose the bloody kids too. Oh my God—not my kids. What have I become? I'm as bad as all the rest of these Bastards I have known—which was what I was going to call this book.

I didn't sleep at all that night, just kept tossing and turning and wondering what to do next. What can a person do 25 kms from town with no license. I rang Mr. Hate in the morn' and sheepishly told him of the events of the last evening. It's really a wonder he didn't say I could have told you so, or just hung up. (he's got what he wants) But he came in and got me and Mat drove my car home. Next I rang Pam, she advised me that if Ebony was in the car as well, I could have a call from Family Services. No way, if they take the kids you never get them back. Mr. Hate went home and left me with my dilemma.

I made my decisions real quick—packed 4 bags of clothes and a few other bits and got Mat and his mate to drive me down to the Islands. I was not going to lose my kids. I decided to go back to the Chicken Factory to pay off the fine and I'd stay at Pam's in the meantime (once again) till I got a flat or a house for me and the kids.

I got straight on at Golden Cockerel, but I knew I would. I may have an alcohol problem but I'm a bloody good worker. Pam baby-sat the kids for me and all in all it wasn't too bad.

Mr. Hate rang about the 3rd day that I was there because someone in Lakes Estate told him of my every intention. I really didn't mean to rip his son away from him it just seemed the best solution to me. I had every intention of contacting him once settled.

Pam was going down south for a week or so and she invited him (Mr. Hate) down to help me out, because she needed a house sitter and I would still need a babysitter as well. I didn't really want this but couldn't see an ulterior plan. So there was the Daddy on the scene once again. Nothing much changed, he still loved his son dearly and I was still a confused mess with a problem. Shortly after that it was Christmas so naturally Mr. Hate came down for that. I couldn't deny him Christmas, the 1st one with his son. I also had no intentions of letting him take Elliot away from me that Christmas. It was a tricky state of affairs.

The following week Mr. Hate rang and offered to come down and get me to take me up to Nanango for Court day. It was fairly obvious I'd have no license after the fact. I accepted. It was my first offence but I still got $2000 fine and 2 years suspension. Oh Shit! And huge amounts of it. I was very upset, well agro about the whole issue and stomped out of the Court House like a Bastard. The Duty Solicitor said, "Don't drive Nicky, you'll get life." "Fuck life," I replied, "If I drive over Black Butt Ranges I'll get Death."

I didn't do that of course, I just didn't think I'd get quite that much time or that much fine. I was hoping for $1000 and only one year. Boo-hoo! It now seemed obvious to me that returning to Lakes Estate was not really a good course of action. I would have to stay in Brisbane and keep working. I guess I'd have to get someone else to drive me to work or move to Mt Cotton so I could walk to work.

Back on Lamb Island sitting round the table, we all discussed the best thing to do. I started looking for a place to live from around the work area and back to the Islands. Sharyn, a lady from Lamb had started at Golden Cockerel recently was going to drive me and herself to work in my car. There was bugger all to rent under $150 a week and that was just too much for me to pay alone. There were a couple of houses on the Island for $100 and less but once you add the boat fares you end up in the same boat. Ha! Ha!

The next suggestion came from Mr. Hate and it was to share house and share baby-sitting. Well half of $155.00(the price for the house I'd found) is $77.50 and with no baby-sitter to pay it was a saving of $100 a week. So really to take the daddy on as a friend which he was in the first place, seemed like the best solution. Once again I agreed. I agreed to sharing a house, sharing costs and sharing the small child that we both loved so much.

I found the house and organized all the shit and he put the bond on, in both names. (silly) He probably knew I didn't want that but we must remember he is a male.

For awhile, he lived his life and I lived mine, at least we tried, or maybe I just tried. I left at 5.30am for work and when I got home I was either in "I'm fucked, I'm going to bed," mode or "I'm partying and I'm off, out," Ok? Ok!

Mr. Hate got a cab license and so it then became, I came in and he went out—or he came in and I went back to work. Obviously the kids were there asleep, or just getting home from school or out playing, but between the 2 parents we somehow managed through this time.

I really hated this house though and so did Mr. Hate and when the six months contract came to an end we both wanted out. Mr Real Estate was a good sort of bloke and he knew what we were looking for and in a couple of days he found us this excellent house 2 streets away.

It was a 2-story house on half an acre, which was pretty rare in Redland Bay. It was 2 streets away from the pub in James Street. Oh no, this could be a bad Omen. Nah! It was a really different sort of house, the bloke had built it himself. I thought he must've been waiting for World War III because the bottom half of the house was all besser-blocks and half way up them were a few peep holes or gun holes I thought. The underneath was also big enough to fit a tank or a truck. Then upstairs every window and every opening had huge shutters to pull across—so if you wanted you could turn daytime into nightime. I loved this house. I loved the spot.

The same shit happened here as the last house. Sharyn picked me up and about when I got home Mr. Hate went out Taxi Driving.

On this one particular day another mate, Colleen was picking me up and dropping me because Shaz wasn't well. We both put in our usual hard day's slog and then as we came down James Street we could see up ahead, cars, an Ambulance, fire-engines and cops. Jesus Christ something going on down this Street today. I thought. Colleen said, "That looks like your place Nick." "No couldn't be my place. Wouldn't be my place." As we got closer but still nearly a block away, which is as close as you could get, I started shaking. "It's not—no it's not, it can't be." I was still looking at all the people—neighbors as well. "The whole fucking tops gone—Oh my God! The whole top is gone." I got out of the car and walked across the road and then saw Mr. Hate and Elliot surrounded by Firemen and Police. The whole house had that yellow tape all round, you know the shit. **DO NOT CROSS.**

Once I'd seen Elliot was still alive and I knew the other 2 were still in school I walked over to Mr. Hate and said (quietly) "You were a-fuckin-sleep weren't you?" "No Nick no I wasn't."

The whole fucking place was gone, the whole top deck.

The owner was leaning over the fence crying saying he was just thinking of selling it. Oh no, and to think I would have bought it given the chance. The insurance assessor was at the fence too and he had to work out how much the owner would get back. Then when I was crying to him—I told him of how we'd only been living here for three weeks all up and now everything was burnt and gone. He told me that I might be able to claim on my contents insurance, because you were covered by the insurance for one month. Incredible—maybe there was some hope of getting something back. I had a chat to the cops and the fire blokes and then Stuart and Ebony came home. The poor bastards. Everything we had was gone. All our daggy shitty ol' bits and pieces were all gone.

It was like a movie scene, where the person arrives home and they have the place barricaded off and you're not allowed in till the forensic blokes have done their job. I could not fucking believe it and all I could think was, "He was asleep." He never admitted it though, not to this day. Would you?

What to do, as usual, was the next question. Well the 22ft caravan that I'd had for a few months was parked underneath and almost untouched. It would have to be the home temporarily. I know how blessed I was that Stu and Ebby were at school that day and that Mr Hart had got Elliot out before the furnace took over. Thinking back though I didn't so much think of that but of all that was gone and while I was out earning a quid too.

Guess what Mr. Hate and Elliot had for lunch? Hot chips! At this stage I could think back to how I had ended up here and how come I was working and etc. etc. but what's the point. Everything is gone, time to move on.

I rang Pam. Jimery was there and said "I'll be down in 10 mins, I'll tow you and the van up here to Pammy's, OK." Mr. Hate's Statesman was still parked just outside but it was locked and the keys had melted. When the bloody Plodd finally let us up the stairs to see what was left I realized that everything was melted, even the old fridge. I honestly thought that the fridge would still be standing in the corner of the kitchen, but it looked like a candle that had slithered slowly across the floor and combined itself with the kitchen sink and a few pots and pans. You could see their handles sticking up out of the molten larva.

"I gotta go. I wanna go now, let's get these kids out of here." There was nothing to grab to take with us—just us. Jim got the caravan hooked up and we sorted a few minor details with the Plodd and insurance mob and then left.

Pamalaza, who was living on the mainland again, had already got all the dinner ready for the kids and us and she had also organized with her neighbor, Bernie to put up with us for a few weeks with the Van hooked up to her house. Everyone was so helpful that night. Except me, I wasn't at all. I got drunk, what's new. Getting drunk on this occasion wasn't really a good plan but it's what I do best. I could ignore what was going on around me while I was drinking—especially if it's all BAD.

So next day I thought, I best get up and go to work. There was no point sitting about moping and there was money to be earned. If I lost my job now I really would be in the shit.

Half the work force had already heard about my dilemma. Many of them had bits and pieces to donate, which they would bring in to work tomorrow. To my way of thinking there wasn't much point getting any of it till we had a house to put it in.

After work Mr. Hate and I went house hunting once again. I still needed a place, anywhere I could get a lift to and from work. A couple of days went by and my insurance assessor arrived and said I should be able to get full contents cover because I'd just moved. Bloody excellent. It seems sometimes, but very rarely, I do get lucky and this was one of those times. We had to go down to the burnt remains again—which was pretty horrible, scary too, because I thought it might fall through in some parts. He took heaps of photos and we told him to the best of our knowledge what was what in the wreckage and also wrote lists of what else was in the house.

Next day I went to work and when I arrived home I was hoping, seriously hoping, Mr. Hate may have found a place or at least have a long list of houses to look at. He got home in the cab just after me and said, "Guess what I'm gonna get for my Ivory Chess set, between $5ooo and $7ooo." Then he went on to say, "I'm also gonna get about $15oo for my Guitar. I grabbed him by his long pony-tail and shook the shit out of it. "Fucken Jesus Mr. Hate we've got no home, no beds, no clothes, no nothing at all and you get quotes on your fucking chess set. We can't live in a chess set you stupid, stupid bastard," at that I let go. **"Go on, fuck off to work."**

I had to do some seriously deep breathing after that to calm myself back down. I couldn't believe it. I still can't believe it. His excuse later was that he didn't think I'd want him to get quotes on my stuff. HUH. I didn't either, I just wanted a place to live and put the shit in, it's fairly obvious I would have thought.

On the weekend we stopped at this old farm house near-by which was for sale and inquired about the price etc. While talking to those old people they told us of another old farm house just up the road a bit that was apparently empty. I got a phone number off them and we left.

When I finally got hold of the bloke Mr. Jones, he said it was really old and he wasn't going to put anyone in it again, he intended to bulldoze it. Then I explained to him of the circumstances why we were homeless and he re-considered and arranged a meeting. He liked me immediately, I could tell. After some chit chat I said $65, he said "I was thinking $85 and then I put my hand out for the shake and said $75 he took my hand and the deal was done. Thank Christ for that. We had only been living behind Bernies for three wks but that was more than enough, especially in the confinement of a caravan and with Mr. Hate whom I blamed for the whole issue. OK it could happen to anyone I guess, but I still blamed him, I couldn't help it and I wasn't happy with him to start with so this just gave me a new excuse.

In between all this, my darling Pam had rung the Redland bay school and told them of our family dilemma. The staff at the school and many of the parents had all sorts of donations for us. They gave Pam a call one day and asked could we please come and get the stuff that had been donated. I could not believe my eyes when we got there. I stopped dead, with tears in my eyes, the whole sick room was full, absolutely full of gear. Bags of clothes, boxes of crockery, linen, pillows, kids toys, cutlery, you name it, was in that room. All good quality stuff as well, lots of it brand new. Never before have I felt so overwhelmed with the generosity of the human race. I was dumbstruck.

It took Mr. Hate and I, two trips in the Statesman, which has a huge boot, to get all of the gear back to our van. The van was now completely overflowing so thankfully we were moving into our little farm house by the following weekend. Then came the insurance assessor again, who said all would go ahead and I just had to get two quotes for each item and whichever they thought the most reasonable would be where I would then shop.

Now I could seriously smile again. Wonderful, excellent, marvelous, I was going to get it all back only all New. I'd hardly ever bought anything new. We went to Captain Snooze and to A-mart for quotes for the furniture, to Big W for the bits and pieces and to Retravision for all the electrical. By the following week we started to see some results.

The gorgeous new 4 piece lounge suite in mottled grey arrived, followed by the dining suite and the entertainment unit and a few other various tables and children's cupboards all from A Mart. A couple of days later was the delivery from Retravision. I had picked the flashiest fridge I could find with quick freeze setting (to get that beer cold) and a digital clock in the front. It was a new for old policy so my dirty, rusty $50 fridge became this frost free 900l beauty. Then all the new appliances:—jug, toaster, breville, scales, barbie grill etc. The T.V. and the video and CD player were all Mr. Hate's and so by now his insurance company had joined forces with mine and then I s'pose they could halve the end result. Cheeky bastards.

Anyway I furnished the whole place at Redland Bay to start with and Mr. Hate put in nothing, so I figure what's mine is mine and that's that. Last but definitely not least came the bedroom suite. I had just bought a queen size four poster (made of aluminum) bed with all the lacey curtains for $120.00 in a second hand shop at Cleveland. This was valued at nearly $2000 new so therefore I had 2 grand worth of bed with all the matching pieces with lead light around the mirror of the dutchess and lead light roses in the bed head, as well as 2 side tables. Absolutely gorgeous.

Everything slowly fell into place and as I've said this was apparently, "The best thing that ever happened to me". Well I'm bloody well hoping that the publishing of this book will change people's thoughts on that, because as far as I'm concerned, it was one of the worst things that ever happened. (at this point)

I had a lot of arguments with Mr. Hate at this time and I still did not love him and it wasn't gonna change. I asked him to move out after about a month or so and off he went to Pam's old house at Capalaba, and Pam moved up to Maryborough.

I was happy with the "farm house" and I was happy with all the lovely new gear and I didn't even mind Golden Cockerel so much, but then as life goes on, shit happens, this time in the form of health problems. I got Carpel Tunnels. This is a condition many believe to be a load of ol' cobblers, but I had it so I know it's true. My wrists and arms were fine all day while working flat out, but at night they don't stop. It's like pins and needles sort of, but you can't get any sleep. No matter which way you lie the arms are still annoying you. Hanging them over the side of the bed seemed best. No lying on them, no shaking them about. No, nothing works in the end, bar an operation.

So I was to have an operation on both wrists at once. This is the best way as they both recover together and you can get back to work. Thank Christ I'd paid my fine off before this.

Again Mr. Hate had to be around. He was absolutely wonderful at this time—he did everything. He had no choice in the matter anyway. I was completely useless for a couple of weeks. Couldn't even hold a beer. You can imagine my horror at that.

It was toward the end of my Compo time and I went out partying like I love to do. While slithering down the gutter outside the Alex Hills Tav. Cab driver 188 (Mr. Hate) pulled up and I jumped the 400 odd people in the queue to my own private CAB. Mr. Hate took me back home and then I invited him in. That's one free lift home.

Wam Bam thank-you Mam. I was pregnant again. Oh shit. Oh double shit. Now what do I do?. I'd just got my own life back again and here I was the stupid drunk and preggers again at 36 years of age. Will I ever learn? Will I have another baby to Mr. Hate? It was hard enough convincing him before that I couldn't love him and wouldn't live with him. Once again I could abort and once again I knew, I had always wanted a big family. Nothing would ever be as I had wanted it though and those were childish dreams and this was the real thing.

I was booked in to one of those horrible illegal places to have the VAX job done on myself. I had to stop smoking and drinking and eating for 12 hour before midnight. At precisely midnight, I said to me ol' mate Suey "Fuck the clinic, get me another scotch and a cig will ya." She hugged me and we both cried. I was having my fourth child.

Needless to say Mr. Hate was wrapped once again about this turn of events. Well as we know I really did want six children and I'll not change it now. Here we go again. It was close this time. I love the feeling of the pregnancy it's just the other person that I can't seem to get it right with.

"This will be the last time, I know it is the last time, maybe it's the last time, but I don't know."

That was the last time and I do know. This time I got my tubes tied **AS WELL.**

When I was about 6 months pregnant, Mr. Hate came in to the shower room and stood the other side of the shower curtain and said, "I s'pose we should get married now." I don't s'pose the silly cunt even realized that was a question, let alone a marriage proposal. Well it was not a proposal to me. The fact that you've had one, two, or three kids does not a marriage make. I'm sure as well that love was meant to come in to the scenario somewhere, but these days it's not so. Kids come first so often and love maybe comes later. I still hope for that.

I remember this time quite well. I wasn't working and the pregnancy was taking it out of me more, as I was getting older. I went to go for an hour's sleep and asked Ebby to watch out for Elliot while I did so. Pam was there as well so was Stuart so between all them I thought Elliot would be fine. No I was wrong. I woke up to, "Where's Elliot, Where's Elliot?"

I wouldn't even mention this part of the story only it makes you understand my feelings for Mr. Hate a bit better. Well Elliot was not on the house yard and he had never before gone past the big chook shed, that was his line that he wasn't allowed past. Any way we were all yelling out for him and he wasn't there, not anywhere. Pam rang Mr. Hate on the Taxi mobile and told him and in the meantime I ran up and down the road and up the next hill—fell over a couple of times and then some neighbors told me the safe house had him and they'd bring him back to my home in a minute. Thank God, and I'm not religious. Thank God. Mr. Plodd brought my baby boy home. Someone had found him at the bottom of our driveway, but because it was so overgrown it didn't look like any one lived there and so they took Elliot away.

Well I thought he was gone. I really thought that my afternoon nap was the end of my third child. It was not like that though, and Elliot was brought back to me. Mr. Hate did come racing home too—because Pam had rung him about the dilemma. He stopped long enough to have a cuppa and a joint and then said "I best get back to work!"

Well I never. I was still a quivering mess. He could not even hug me. He could not offer any warmth or compassion. He just best get back to work. Well he'd had **HIS FUCKIN JOINT NOW!**

I was a mess for the next week or probably month or so. I nearly lost one of my bubbas. Mr. Hate didn't care. He didn't give a fuck about the one in the belly either. If I was in shock and had gravel rash from arsehole to breakfast he wouldn't have even known. Elliot was alive—time to go back to work. BYE.

This of course got to me and I could not let it go by. **FUCK OFF MR. HATE. YOUR LOVE FOR ME IS SO FUCKING BORING. THE KIDS STILL ALIVE AND YOU CAN GO NOW.**

Why was he here at all—because he can drive, because I have no license—and because he's the only Daddy out of 3 that even looked back?

Mr. Hate did, of course, return and he did continue to piss me off as I'm sure I did him, but towards the end of the pregnancy we got a bit closer, as I s'pose Mummas and Puppas should. Finally the time came and Mr. Hart was there to drive me to the hospital, which I made damn sure of.

When we got to the Logan Hospital the staff asked me, "What do you want to help with the birth". "I want the bloody lot this time, this is my fourth and last baby and I want it all." I got it too, just not the epidural. The young lass came into the labour room at one stage and asked, "Who turned this gas up?" I answered, "I fucken did. After all, I'm the one in labor." They left me alone after that. Mr. Hate was there as he would be and at around 9.30am another perfect little baby boy was born to me.

My parents came up to visit later on that day. I had decided to call this little fella Larry, after my own wonderful father, and nothing would stop me. I also decided that this child was going to be a Brett, my family name. Mr. Hate was pissed off about this, but who gives a rats. I already had a Mc Farlane, a Norden, a Hart and this one is bloody well mine. My little Larry Brett. Larry the last.

Once again I was happy but not necessarily with Mr. Hate, just with my life and my newborn. Now that there was one more the old farm house didn't really suit any more and the crunch came about a month later. I'd broken my foot while out and about with Lois Lane.

Mr. Hate was everything my parents wanted, I reckon. This was gonna be it this time though, because he was nothing to me or to mine. After another month or so I just wanted to run again. I hated this old house now. There wasn't enough room really. I kept hoping that Mr. Hate would do something about it. He didn't. When the snake showed its ugly head out of the pantry, I shit myself and then I rang Mr. Hate's work. He wasn't there and he was busy, obviously making heaps of money to support his woman and kids, huh! So his boss and some other bloke came and sorted that problem and I just wanted out.

He was actually living in a caravan up at the wood place at this stage and I thought he'd find a nice place for us all now I'd decided to move again. He didn't. As usual it was down to me to make all the decisions and organize a new house.

I could've gone home to Nanango at this time, but my parents were still on the Island and I didn't want to go to far from them till they were sorted out. Dad had Parkinsons Disease and they had to move off the Island because it was all becoming to hard what with the boats.

Well Eagleby looks cheap. Lois lives there too. Good plan Naughty Nickers. Let's all go to Eagleby. It's still not too far up the highway and over to the Islands. All the places I looked at round Redland Bay were $160-$190 and all the places at Eagleby were round $100-$130ish. I finally found an excellent place in a cul-de-sac which was on two blocks so we had a huge back yard for the 2 dogs to run and for the Kids' swings and trampolines etc.

It was only three minutes to the local shops, the closest op shop and of course the All Sports Club. Beauty, if' I do wish to go out I won't have a problem driving home because I won't drive down there. It's only three bucks in a cab. How easy can you get?

The house was a grand change to the ol' farm-house, it was all modern and everything was clean and easy. The laundry was inside and the back door went from the laundry straight to the line as you would expect. How simple. It had a nice big lounge and all my new furniture looked a whole lot better in a flashy new house. The dining suite looked nice just through the archway and beyond that was a nice, neat, concreted pergola area with a proper barbie. Then the huge yard nicely scattered with tall gums and other plants. I loved it here. Life was good. No, life was great.

Mr. Hate decided he was gonna take a flat in the area, because he was sick of Sam Arnold (Benedict) ripping him off and he wanted to be near the boys. So very shortly after I moved, Mr. Hate took a two bedroom flat about four blocks away and opposite the Civic Sports Club.

Fine, bloody well fine, do what you like Mr F . . . Hart, I'm going to live my life now. You can't look after me and what's more you won't. He could have found a place first, like a man and perhaps I would have moved in with him again, but he didn't.

I became a bit of a regular at the Club, mainly on Wednesday Nights for the Karaoke, and Friday nights for the raffles. One night while clubbing it I won three meat trays in a row. Good shit. I had meat for at least a month and other than that Mr. Hate was there that night and he could whip the meat over to his fridge, while taking his young sons home and I could party on. Stu and Ebby were at home but I felt they were quite safe with Bronsan the Pit Bull and Araloon the Great Dane to protect them.

It became one of those wonderful places like "Cheers", where *"everybody knows your name"*. I like it like that, I could walk in and at least 10 people would say, "Hi Nick, how ya going." Perch yourself on a stool for a couple of hours, meet a few new folks, dance a jig, tell a joke or two and finally stagger home or get the boys in a cab and go home from there

I was just really enjoying myself. Sometimes Mr. Hate would turn up in the morning to bring the boys home and come in for a cuppa. No problems. For an Ex, he had the most access to his children than anyone else I've ever known. We were friends. Maybe even best friends. By the way I was still sleeping with him once every so often, probably once a fortnight or so. Well I couldn't slut around and I couldn't live with Mr. Hate so this was the best way for me.

Not really too bad of a set up, I thought. I still had all the responsibilities and all the bullshit house work and the two older kids which were becoming a handful and he—Mr Hart could just go home if the going got tough or if he was too tired to contend with all that. I felt I had it pretty good and so did he. Why upset this perfectly balanced relationship. A Claytons relationship really. If only I could do that with the Grog instead of the relationship. Can't though, don't want to either.

Right, well it was at this time the Urvan, my latest vehicle started to play up. By the way I had my license back by now, finally and I didn't have to rely on Mr. Hate anymore. Anyway the Van always had a slight problem with the starter motor, so that was the first thing to be replaced. Then it turned out it was not the starter motor at al,l but the flex plate or ring gear. Before I had the chance to replace this I blew up the muffler one morning trying to start it. That cost me $85.00.

Then when going to a kid's party one day I ran into James again, James from Nanango. I gave him my address and a few days later he turned up. He was amusing to me, another Jarmas, almost an exact replica, only not black and not Ebony's Dad. He was gonna stay a while and fix my car. He was only staying on the lounge. Good shit, like I said he was amusing. We went to the club a couple of times and he stayed and fucked round with the car a couple of days and Mr. Hate turned up earlier and earlier each morning to say hi, whether he had the boys or not. We had borrowed his tools too, but I got sick and tired of him assuming the worst and told him to fuck off and take his tools with him. He did.

Then I introduced James to Suey, because I just knew they'd hit it off—which they did! I'm not sure how the next bit quite came about but suddenly James was moving in with Mr. Hate—into his spare room which wasn't quite done up for the boys yet. (sarcasm) he did have a mattress on the floor for himself and one for them too. No worries really on my part, just sorta pissed me off a bit because the Urvan never quite got fixed **that** day.

CHAPPIE 16

The next sequence of events ended up in an affidavit and in court eventually, with the drama and stress it caused me followed by the biggest drama of all time.

It started with the wonderful $3000 Urvan which Mr. Hate's boss (Taxi) found for me back before I had Larry. It was never bloody right and I always thought that his boss was doing the favor not for Mr. Hate and I but for his other mate. I also thought it was overpriced but I had some insurance left and urgently wanted a car before I got my license back. Two years is a long time.

I will admit that I was very happy with it for awhile, but all that while someone else was driving it, and not me. Once I finally got my license back the Urvan was near fucked. It helps if the driver glances at the temperature gage occasionally. Anyhow after a certain person boiled it dry it was never any good again.

First it just blew the muffler, because it took so long to start the fumes built up in the muffler and it **BLEW-KA-BOOM!** So it wasn't going, from the 11ᵗʰ of July till the 15ᵗʰ. Sue picked me up for the kid's party and dropped us all home after the weekend. I bought another muffler and got that job done—$85.00.

In the meantime Mr. Hate and James cruised round together in Mr. Hate's safe and well running Mazda 929 which he had got with his insurance. On the 17th the van shit itself again, which was the flexplate and more money. It was still not right but I could actually drive it if I had the strength to turn the motor round a bit manually. Then it broke down again at Lois's place just round the road. A mate of Lois's came round and had a look at it. Apparently none of the bolts had been done up even finger tight and he reckoned it was a wonder the whole lot didn't fall out on the deck! He tightened everything up and said I should be right now and if I ever wanted work done to come and see him. If I come and see him I'll never have to return because he does such a good job. Then it seemed right for awhile, till the 19th anyway.

The next day I got a major service at K Mart Auto so everything was safe. Another $139.00 later, I drove about 10klms and the car shit itself again just in the worst spot you can imagine at rush hour. Typical. I was trying to push it the 10 meters to a servo when some bloke yelled out, "Do you need some help." What sort of a complete fuckwit are you, is what I wanted to yell out but I didn't, and the two of us got it to the servo. All this while streams of traffic are tooting and beeping and swearing out the window while we're pushing it across the oncoming traffic. I rang Mr. Hate. He and James came and got me and the kids once again and dropped us home.

In the morning Mr. Hate took me back to the van and Mr. K Mart Auto came and fixed it again. They did all sorts of checks and grease and oil change etc. and left a nearly broken frayed bit of wire inside the points which had simply broken off. So I'm going again—no charge.

The following weekend Sue and I decided to go to her cousin's 30th up in Kilcoy, about 250kms from home. The van was best because all the seats fold down to make a double bed. We went alone and Mr. Hate had the boys for the weekend. Sue's other cousin stayed at her home in Brisbane with her kids and Ebony stayed there with them. Stuart, now 15 stayed home alone, which he seems to like best.

Sue and I were on a mission, a mission to party. The van went great all the way—no probs at all. We got to outback Kilcoy and in to it. We danced, we drank, we ate and we partied till the wee hours of the morning. There was an all girl band called Black Rose who were bloody excellent and all in all it was a damn good night. When morning came and it was time to think about going I went over to warm up the car and it wouldn't start. It was completely dead. No lights were left on either, or radio, nothing like that, but alas! It was completely dead . . .

We got another battery out of someone's car and tried that. Then Sue called their cousins back from town to have a look at it. I told her not to bother, I'd had enough. Leave the heap of shit there, we'll hitch hike home or walk, or bum a lift off someone and then I can blow the heap up. "Settle down Nick", It'll be all right, we'll get it going again." Bullshit I thought. I had lost the plot. I was still pretty hazy from the night before. The best thing I could think of to do was have a beer! Sue said, "Go for it Nick, I'll drive home anyway."

I had quite a few beers and the day went slowly by. A few different people came and went and a few different people did something to the van and still it would not go. I was beyond the point of caring and had another beer. Then Sue organized us a lift home to Brizzy. We'll have to leave the Urrrrr-van here and sort that out later.

I think it was about 2ish, I couldn't be sure. I just wanted to go home. All I wanted was to just go home and curl up in my own little beddy byes and cry and cry and cry, (I'm crying now) and then cry some more. Me whole life is a shambles. Nothing works. The cars fucked again, the washing machine shit itself again and beside any of this I'm so fucking depressed and I just wanna go home. I really wished there was someone who would come along and fix it all up. But first I just needed a great big hug from someone who cared and there wasn't anyone. I went home.

Home to Nanango. To my home. To all that I had done, which wasn't bloody much, but I needed this. I had to go home. I just kept walking and walking but I had my thumb out as well and I had my big criminal looking jacket on and a beer in my hand, and I was still crying and just kept thinking about it all—all that I wanted and hoped for and what I'd got. AND Mr heart couldn't have given me a big hug if he was fucking well there because he's incapable of showing any sort of emotion or feeling what so fucking ever. More crying. Then finally a lift.

Deep breaths Nick, deep breaths. He was a breath of fresh air too and amazingly enough, someone who cared. The guy was a Jehovas Witness (which he did not shove down my throat) and he was also; unbelievable but true; going to Nanango. Just past it actually. So he dropped me at the Fitzroy—the scene of the crime, and guess what? I got a beer. Then I rang Dave, my tenant and he told me he and Tommy would be in, in about an hour or so and not to cry. They came and got me and Dave gave me a big hug. Bloody hell, things were looking up. Then they took me home.

They were all very kind people, the Christian type that will help people no matter who they are. Like me. Not a practicing Christian going to Church and stuff, just people who care. We've all got a story and we've all got our own reasons. I was just so glad to be home on my verandah, looking out at what I had accomplished. But I was alone. I was always alone. Even surrounded by people and wondering all the time where on earth was my mate, my Mr Right. I knew it wasn't Dave, though I did think he was capable, but he already had a wife and child. He was the sort, a man who could do a bit of everything, a worker, a jack of all trades and master of most. Oh well all the good ones are gone.

I spent the night whinging and crying and taking lots of deep breaths. I figured I was almost at nervous break-down level. The next day I pulled myself together and rang Sue. Sue said, "Everything's cool with Ebony and you just take your time." Then I rang Mr. Hate who said he and James were coming to Nanango next weekend. Christ I couldn't believe him. He thought this was great. He had the boys and I'd lost the plot and taken the wrong direction home. He was also not coming till he was good and ready. Huh! the shit head. He had a mate to play with and to help him and he had his precious boys. I was all depressed again. What was I gonna do now. Dave came over and hugged me and said, "Don't worry Nick we'll go get the car soon. I'll get it going. Still he's hugging me. Allison didn't seem to mind and she trusted him and it was a friendly thing to person in need.

All the way down to get the car I couldn't seem to pull myself together. I felt bad for involving these poor people in my dramas. Dave kept saying it's OK Nick It'll be Ok. After a short 15 mins the wonderful Dave had action stations, the car burst into life. I couldn't believe it. Unreal, he actually got it going. I wanted to drive but I really wasn't capable. I was a nervous drained out wreck. Dave drove the van back with Allison and me while Tommy and Christine went in their car.

I s'pose I should've pulled myself together and driven directly home to the kids, but I couldn't. I didn't want to yet. I was not ready to face Mr. Hate like this. I wished he'd just fucking get in there and do his job or fuck-off. The van was only partially fixed anyhow and Dave was going to go over the whole thing and get it running right for me. Excellent Hey?

All day the next day he worked on the car and did all sorts of jobs including the filing down of some part on the flex-plate again and re-fitting it. Then he did another tune-up and a few other things and then last of all we needed a starter motor. Do you think we could get one anywhere? Pam and Ray even came down from Maryborough with three different ones and none of them fitted. Dave ended up having to do a botch job on the starter and the car was now going again by the 26th, so I was ready to go. I had a couple of golds on the verandah for the last time and then I was on my way home to all my babies. I had a few golds on board and got lights at the Fitzroy on the way out. I was happy. Not happy to be going back to Eagleby, or to Mr. Hate, but happy the car was allright now and I could please myself again and be independent with my family. Ya gotta remember it was 2 whole years of relying on Mr. Hate and his taxi, or on someone else and their time schedule. Since then the bloody car had been one problem after another, but finally I was gonna be allright!

I was cruising along playing all my favourite Bob Dylan numbers, feeling pretty darn good about things again. I was going to go to Mr. Hate's flat to pick up the boys and then go home to my part time residence and seriously think of what I'm doing and what to do next. I had to change something about my life. It was Mr. Hate, I knew that, I'd always just tried to keep things running smoothly with Daddy no three because I didn't and don't want for the two little boys to miss out on their Daddy as Ebony and Stuart had. I just didn't love him, he wasn't the right one for me. I don't believe that he ever loved me anyway. He just loved his perfect baby boy and was never going to let him go. Now of course this was twice over.

What a bloody dilemma I'd got myself in. The two older kids couldn't stand him and he had never bothered much with them either, but why should he—there not his. I don't love anyone else's kids as much as mine so how can I expect it of some Bloke!

More shit happened. The van shit itself 20 minutes from home at the last toll-bridge. Something went clunk! In the motor area and then I hit the toll road ramp thingo and got a flat as well. Great, fucking great!

I tried to change the tyre but couldn't see too well and could not budge the nuts on the wheel. I threw the wheel brace back in the van and grabbed my bag and headed off down the highway. I got to Kingston exit, about 4lms and thought I'd ring Mr. Hate. This did not impress me, not at all. I was fuming that I'd broken down again and could not help myself, but I was much more fuming about having to ring Mr. Hate. So I rang Sue and explained where I was and if she couldn't pick me up to then ring Mr. Hate. So I sat on the wall and waited. I waited and waited. I had climbed up on a brick wall at the back of the Garage so I could see all.

Mr. Hate pulled slowly into the garage facing towards the wall. I thought he'd seen me. He drove round the pumps, sort of slowly and I started to climb down the wall. He slowly drove off as I threw my handbag at the boot of his car, which missed and he continued off out of the garage and down the highway again. FUCK FUCK FUCK! I couldn't believe it. I just did not fucking believe it. He'd come and he'd gone. He'd gone again and I was still here and still completely fucked and I still have to get HOME.

I walked back down the highway towards home and after a bit of a walk a cab went by so I grabbed it (which I should have done to start with) I was bawling again and asked the cabbie how much to Eagleby and he said, "about $30.00." I went to check my bag and then I realised my wallet was not in there but obviously still in the bloody van back at the toll bridge. The bloke didn't believe me at first but after a few minutes he could tell this was no Bullshit. He drove back to the toll which you have to go through and then turn round to get over to my van. Then his cab died in the arse. Just stopped. Stopped and wouldn't go again. **Unbelievable.** It is true though. I started crying again. The fare was $15.50 already and I still wasn't gonna get home. I told the Cabbie I'd get his money out of the van and come back in a sec. He said "Just forget it love, just get yourself home." I'll call you another cab." "No don't bother mate." I just walked off, in sort of shock, I couldn't believe my luck. I was back where I started from. I started walking again after grabbing the last three cans of heavy and my wallet. After another half-hour or so someone pulled over and gave me a lift nearly to home. Then I had the last half-hour to walk.

As I walked this last leg of my long journey, I got faster. I got more pissed off with Mr. Hate. Firstly for not stopping at the Kingston garage to ask the bloke if I was about and secondly for everything else. Faster and faster I went and more and more angry. About the first baby and the 2nd and all the shit in between. I know it was my own fault for being a drunk but it didn't stop me feeling used and taken advantage of, by an old man at that. He knew what he was doing, he always knew what he was doing. He was just going to keep following me till I went completely insane and then he'd got what he wanted.

Pam even used to say it to me, "He'll give you enough rope, so you could hang yourself."

Well I've had it he's not getting any more of my easy going 'let's be friends' sort of attitude, he can get fucked. He can see the boys once a fortnight like all the other Ex-Husbands and Boyfriends and De-factos. He's ruining my life. He makes our family unit part down the seam, instead of combining together like a family should. He also makes sure if there's anyone at all half keen on me, he makes out we're together and starts saying "Oh we did this, and **WE** did that". But really **"HE"** is going **backwards** and **"HE"** is **boring** and **"HE"** is getting **out** of my personal life.

By the time I got to his front door I was absolutely frothing at the mouth. AT him and at all of my fucked up life. I smacked him round the face, I smacked his face from side to side and side to side again, saying, "You fucking stupid idiot, you didn't even try to find me or look for me. You didn't even stop, are you trying to push me over the edge of sanity."

I was so agro I couldn't stop myself. Then Mr. Hate went and grabbed Larry out of his room. This made me more angry because he'd brought my own son into a major drama situation to protect himself and he held Larry up close around his face. I started throwing things across the room then—anything I could grab off the table I threw. Nothing Audrey Hepburn wouldn't do. Then Mr. Hate said "James, James you'll have to come out here and help me." Jesus Christ, what sort of a man is this. He'd get his woman basher mate to come out and help him.

Well his woman basher mate rang the cops instead and about an hour later after me just slithering down the wall and saying "Who gives a fuck, then Mr. Hate will get what he wants." They arrived. I didn't want to go with them and I'd come back and get my kids in the Morning. It didn't matter because while they were standing at Mr. Hate's flat door He said, "She hit me while I was holding the baby." This would just make it worse for me as well. The little fucker could open his gob to put shit on me but he could never seem to open it to make things allright. Never, not in nearly 5 years.

So the bloody police took me away to Beenleigh Watch House for the next four hours and that was the end to my wonderful trip home with my newly fixed car. Home to my children. I stayed awake the whole time, thinking about it all. I couldn't believe I was here. After all the violent shit that has happened to me and now Mr. Hate had me locked up for smacking him and smashing some plates. It wasn't really Mr. Hate, but he let it happen and he also tried to make it worse. He didn't try to defend me. He was glad. Maybe he had set me up to send me over the edge after all.

Finally they let me go and I paid 20 cents and the cop told me my friend Sue would be outside in a minute. When she did arrive she had fucking James in the car. Bullshit. I wasn't getting in at first—but I was so sick of walking, I just got in the back between the kids. Her kids. We went back to her house, I don't know why but we did. They got out and I stayed where I was. Then I got out and walked off and screamed out **"You're a DOG James, you're a fucking dog."** I left to walk home yet again. Sue came after me and convinced me to have a cone and a coffee and she would take me home to get the boys. "I've still gotta get my shit box off the highway."

"We'll work it out Nick." I really was losing it, but I just wanted to get my boys and Ebby and Stu and be normal again and go home—without Mr. Hate.

I got part of that wish. Mr. Hate rang later that day and said, "I've gone away with the boys for the weekend to think about things and I'll ring Monday." He only spoke to Sue and I had no chance to speak to Mr. Hate at all. Sue convinced me to stay there not to go home alone and she would go get the Urvan with James. James explained to me he thought it was in every one's best interest that I was locked up for my own good. He reckoned I would have hurt myself or someone else as agro as I was. I decided to forgive him.

I still sat on the verandah then, in Sue's hammock and cried, I don't know why but I just couldn't stop *crying, crying, crying, cry-ing over you cryyyying over you and so now you're gone, I am standing all alone, alone and crying, crying, crying.* It was still to me Jarmas that was the one who was GONE—so to speak, but I felt so much love for him and I'd never ever felt the same since. Well there was Hippy Lee but it was so short lived that I got over it fairly quickly. Or did I?

Maybe I'd never had time enough to get over any of it. Being a drunk didn't help I know, but Jesus Christ did they (MEN) have to take advantage of someone so low. **Everytime.** Someone so open and honest. Someone so desperate, so lonely. The answer is yes, **because they're men. They have to use every diabolical thing that they can come up with to score and to keep scoring, usually with as little effort as possible.**

Well thanks for not coming. Mr. Right is not coming and he's never been, so it's about time I bloody got on with it and stopped missing Mr half way wrong. You know who he is don't ya?

Right, well I had it all sorted in my tiny mind that I'd be the one to succeed and they could all go get knotted.

Later Sue got the kids from school as well like she had been doing each day without complaint. James went out to get the car after that and it was brought back on a tow truck. There goes another 60 bucks. I just wanted to blow the heap up even more than last week.

Mr. Hate rang—he wouldn't speak to me. Sue listened—the look on her face was not good. No—it was horror. She got off the phone.

"He's not coming back Nick. He's thought about it and he's not coming back. **He's keeping the Boys".** He is keeping **my** boys. Those fucking words will never, ever quite go from my mind and neither could I write them or say them without falling apart. (gotta wipe me eyes now the kids are coming) Oh my God—he's keeping the boys. The boys, who are they. I thought Elliot and Larry were their names. They very quickly became the Boys. No one else ever mattered. As if I didn't already know. We all knew. Me and Stu and Ebby always knew. He showed so openly his love and affection for his boys and was so clammed up when it came to us three. After all I was a big fat ugly and now viscous drunk and who could blame him. Who could blame any of them. I didn't want any of them anyway, so I'd be right mate. I am Mr. Right.

Not my babies, he can't take the babies. He has though. Not like Jarmas, he wasn't up the road somewhere—playing a game; he was gone, with my Elliot and my little tiny Larry. I'd bashed him like

Jarmas had bashed me and I'd been away fixing the car (or fixing my soul) and now he's run off. Maybe he was even scared. Jesus Christ what have I become—what have I done. Why am I so fucked up? I don't deserve any of it anyway—fuck it all. They are all better off without me. Stuart would be wrapped. Jarmas and Ebony would be wrapped and Fucking Mr. Hate is already wrapped. So why the fuck am I here. There's no use whatever any more for me so I can just fuck off and everyone will be happy.

No. I could never do it. Never will I. I'll fight and I'll fight every time, till the end. They are my bloody kids and I love em' in my way and I'll bring them up the best way I can with all my faults and downfalls. No one is ever taking my KIDS. MINE!

So I snapped out of my misery a bit and got an attitude that was only thanks to Sue. Who listened to all my moaning and crying and all my despair. We have to get up and keep going. I have to, it's not just Elliot and Larry I have to remember, it's Stu and Ebby too. They'd all be better off I think sometimes but I must prove that to be wrong. These first 2 born don't know their fathers and their fathers don't know them. As for the last 2, this bastard is not getting away with this, no way. Those two little boys are going to be raised by their Mother. I've tried and always will to do my best for us all. (I hope this book is a goer)

Sue was a tower of strength at this time in my life. She may never know how much I love and appreciate her till she reads these words. I would not have survived without her. We all go our own ways at times but a true friend will be there when you're as fucked up as I was. You need them. No return expected. Nothing at all expected—they just want to drag you through in your hour of need and hope you will be there for them. AND if you're not they'll still love YA Unconditional Love they call it. It's great with friends. Not so great with lovers. turning the other cheek just gets it knocked off, in my experience.

Saturday morning around 4.30am I decided to ring Malinda's place. I knew she was s'posed to go up to her new place in Nanango but now without Mr. Hate and or James to help out, or me with my Urvan I just thought maybe Mr. Hate was there. After about four rings it answered and then I said "Hello it's me, Nicky." The phone was hung up. I thought that must be Mr. Hate. Malinda's hiding him out at her place. I rang again and the phone was off the hook.

"Wake up Sue—quick wake up—Mr. Hate's probably at Lyns Bags. No one's s'posed to be there and the phone was picked up and put back down and now it's engaged. Quick lend me the car. I won't be long."

Sue really didn't wanna trust my driving at the moment so she got up and we zapped over to Malinda's place straight away. Someone had left there in an awful hurry. It had rained all night and there were definite tyre tracks in the driveway, small car, tyre tracks. There was a whole pile of tapes on the verandah like they were ready to go; and a garbage bag full of stale bread—obviously to go to the animals up there in Nanango. Nothing seemed to fit, but I was positive Mr. Hate had left from here just before we arrived.

I stayed at Sue's again, she didn't really trust me on my own at this stage. I wasn't so sure myself. I cried all night.

I absolutely had to pull myself together or I would have nothing left to pull myself together for.

Monday morning Sue took me down to Beenleigh to pay all the bills. My house payment, three weeks rent and the phone bill and the Austar and afterward I met them (her and James) back at the pub. (This alone could have been one huge mistake but it was just where I met them.) Malinda rang while we were there and James answered. I didn't give it a thought at that moment. James said, "Yeah, we're all at the Sundowner having a scotch." Mr. Hate's mobile again. This of course sounds like no one at all gives a fuck (ME) and we're all out at the pub enjoying the day. Well that was so far from the truth, it hurt. I couldn't believe the pain I was in. The pain this little horrible man, was putting me through. After all I'd tried to do, to give him as much access and friendship and normality around HIS kids as was possible after the relationship break-down.

How could he do this to me. The amount of times I just wanted him to go away and visit once a fortnight. I always just said "Oh hi Mr. Hate." And Elliot would come running ou,t "Oh Daddy, Daddy's here yeah! So then, I just invite him in for a cuppa and we'd have a bit of a chat and just be friends—like we used to be and like parents should always try to be. This went on until he'd slowly push his way back in and I'd eventually lose it and tell him to go home. A few days later the same scenario. Until I'd really lose it and then he'd stay away for a week.

I was trying to be fair all round really. To my older kids who did not like Mr. Hate, to the younger two who love their Daddy, and of course to Mr. Hate, who I now realized could not live without them. Where did I fit in, just keeping everyone else happy. What about me? I could not live without my kids either, but I could not live with Mr. Hate. It was a bastard situation and now it's finally blown up. Well I blew up really, I guess. Still; I'm not in the **NUT HOUSE, Yet. Close.**

I rang everyone on the planet I could think of from home that night to ask about his whereabouts. No-one I mean No-one had seen or heard from him. I kept in touch with James on a very regular basis in case he heard from Mr. Hate. He was also under strict instruction to beg and plead with Mr. Hate to ring me. None of this happened. Mr. Hate and my two sons had disappeared without a trace.

Next day got worse. Sue, James and I were discussing what to do or try next when the cops arrived at the front gate. "You don't have to accept anything Nicky." Sue said. I didn't really know what she meant, but if I don't accept they can't take me to court, I think. They were handing me a **PROTECTION ORDER and Temporary Sole Custody Order** that I stay and have no contact with :-

John Richard Mr. Hate Hart
Elliot Alvis Hart
Larry Ernest Brett

No contact at all with my sons, a protection order—I passed out. I came round again and James and Sue had me inside. You've got no idea the grief and turmoil inside me. No one could. Little innocent Nicky, who wanted a whole bed full of babies and one Mr Right, has a protection order from seeing the babies, her own little babies. "I wasn't trying to hurt them," I spat out. "I wasn't trying to hurt them at all. It's him that's driving me mad. Him. That dirty little bastard." I had the shakes, as well as bursting into tears at the drop of a hat and every so often my whole body would just shudder and twitch out of control. I was a mess. How long is this torment going to last. I can't bear the pain. How long is this man who professes to love me going on with this torture. **This terrible, horrible torture.**

Stuart and Ebony were in pain too and God only knows what the little boys were thinking. I can't know because I don't know where they are. **I just don't know where my 2 little boys are.** How dare you do this to me Mr Hart, I yelled and screamed out the pain. "How dare you." No phone calls still.

Nothing at all and no phones calls to anyone he knew, nothing all the next day. We now knew he'd got as far as Hervey Bay because that was where the Protection Order had come from. "I have to find him, I have to find him and talk to him." Next move was to get a vehicle and find the Bastard. Fuck the courts. I ended up hiring a car with my tax return money and James offered to drive me round the planet to look for him.

I couldn't use this money to get my urvan fixed now there wasn't time. I had to go Now, as soon as humanly possible, and find my kids. Who knows what is going through Mr. Hate's head. I must find him before it's too late. This is the best way. We've always talked it out before. He had it pretty good I thought. Oh Fuck where is he.

We drove all over the planet and asked after Mr. Hate. We went out to Nanango and then across to Hervey Bay. His best mates in Hervey Bay said they had not seen him and so did friends at Nanango but I didn't believe a living soul any more. I had to find him. Still after nearly two days of searching all the places I could think of, still No

Mr. Hate and No Babies. I had spent all my excess money and failed. Home again to Eagleby, empty handed and empty hearted.

Oh that Bastard! Still no calls, no contact. Nothing.

The next days were taken up with court and court houses, the filling out of many forms, seeing solicitors and Women's Legal Services and anything else I could possibly do to get my Elliot and Larry home with the rest of the Family, OUR Family. Nothing quite made it to the result I wanted. If I could have got the EX-Parte paper into the Family Court before 4pm and with all the other documents to go with, they could maybe get the Police to go and retrieve the children until the pending court case in Hervey Bay which was another bloody week away yet. I didn't quite make it. Do you know how that feels. It's incredibly painful to know that Now on this Friday afternoon of September my kids having been missing for a whole week and there is absolutely nothing at all else I can do till Monday morning. The court is closed. I'm too late. I've missed the boat. I staggered down the Family Court steps in a daze.

Still no babies. I believe I bought a bottle of scotch. I knew it wouldn't help, but it wouldn't hurt either. At least maybe I'd get some sleep at the end of this day.

My dad told me to come over the Island and get his old car and have it. "Just have it Nick and go find your sons". I went over the night before with Ebony and picked up the car and we were booked on the first barge back to the mainland, 5.40am. Missed that and had two hours to wait for the next. The receptionist told me the wrong barge going the wrong way and not to the mainland. I still had time to get all my shit in before the end of this day. Sharon babysat Ebony for me and wrote a character reference as well and off I went, in my new wheels to conquer the world.

Finally it all got through and the judge granted that the children were to reside with me until the next Family Court Proceedings. The judge said that because we still had no idea of Mr Hart's whereabouts she would make it that as I was to see him in the Hervey Bay Court

House, I could serve these Orders to the attending Police Officer at the Magistrates Court, on that day.

This was still too many days away for me but at least I had a lump of paper in my hand which would give my children straight back. This I believe is called an Interim Residency Order, which tops Mr. Hate's bullshit anyway.

The next days went oh so slowly and Mr. Hate never rang. It was two weeks now and he'd not rung, not his Mum, not my Mum, no one at all had heard. We did know that he was still alive though because he wouldn't need a protection order otherwise. Then finally the time came round and Malinda and I and all the kids went up to Pam's on the Thursday night, ready for the big onslaught on the Friday again.

The whole lot of us went in to the courts, Pam came as well for moral support. Finally there he was, seconds before the court hearing. He had not brought Elliot or Larry. I cried. He got closer and he looked really mean. He was rigid with hate and would not speak to either Malinda or Pam. I wasn't s'posed to go near him of course or I'm breaking the law. He was standing in the other room. I walked in and tried to talk. "Fuck off Nicky—it's in my Solicitors hands now." I walked out and sort of kept my decorum, well I had papers to say hand over the kids by 4 o'clock today, or else. HA!

In we went and all the general bullshit happened and I handed my orders to the attending Police Officer and he then gave them to Mr. Hate's Solicitor. I think he was supposed to give them to the Judge. Not knowing enough Fucked me up again.

Any way they granted the Temporary Protection Order and Custody bit and Mr. Hate's Solicitor stuffed him quickly out of the Court House and then he disappeared. I screamed out "Pam quick grab him I can't touch him or I'm done". She bolted up the road after Mr. Hate and grabbed his shirt scratching him down the guts in the process. He slithered out of his shirt and took off and was last seen leaping into the Solicitor's car and they drove off towards Sally's.

That was my thoughts and I got Lyns and all the kids in and set chase towards Sally's as fast as I could go. It was mad I know, but I was completely insane by now, this is 2 weeks without my 1 and 3 year olds, and Larry I'd not long stopped feeding.

It was Dick Johnson eat ya heart out, if you ask me but once again a waste of time. I was wrong, Mr. Hate did not have the kids stashed at Sall's house and so off we went again back to the cop shop where Pam was still trying to tell them I had a Family Court Order to have the kids returned today.

This is not happening. No, it's not happening I was so messed up now, I could hardly breath. "Pam you've gotta tell them. I can't. I'll lose the plot and end up in more shit." Pam did everything—the cops said they had not seen the orders and they had to be served to the Person by a policeman or bailiff. Furthermore it's Friday afternoon and there is no Baliff available at the moment. I don't believe this is happening. I just don't. Something went wrong in that court place and it was a shonky Lawyer at play. He told Mr. Hate to fuck off quick and then handed the papers back to me and they scarpered.

Oh my God! He was gone again. Oh my God. Again I had failed. I was drained. I'd done everything right as rules of Law and Courts go but I just didn't get them served to Mr. Hate by the cop and the cop passed them to the Solicitor who was Mr. Hates mate and knew what he was doing. Fuck.

Pam took over driving after that episode and we drove round all over Hervey Bay and showed photos in every corner of the place, but nothing, still nothing. After that I directed Pam to the bottle shop. I ordered three for $10 ouzo, that's all. Malinda said "You'll never get your boys back if you don't stop drinking". We had a little row and I got my drinks and started drinking them. "Anyway Malinda I wouldn't mind if you would just shut up".

The drive back out to Pams was in silence. I was about to explode and thought it best to just shut up. Malinda had pissed me off through this whole episode anyway—making out Mr. Hate was Mr fucking wonderful and I wasn't all too sure she didn't hide him at her place the first night.

Now I had to wait another whole week for the next appearance in the Family Court which would be the final one.

I was a nervous wreck but I was ready and I was confident with all this shit to put on Mr Hart that I would win. At the same time this was my whole life in his hands and I was terrified. The Man had put me through hell and I was still in pain and still at his mercy. Chris, Sue's bloke, went and spoke to Mr. Hate at my request. I decided that rather than take this final risk we should reconcile. I was too afraid that maybe, just maybe, the courts would turn the kids over to Mr Hart. I could not stand that. I could not possibly live like that. Having to go to Mr. Hate's residence to see my own sons and to be only able to do this once a fortnight. He also had added to his affidavit that these visits should be supervised (I found out later). I could not possibly live like this. I had never made him live through that sort of shit but I was sure and positive if he had the upper hand he would put me through hell, just like he was doing to me right now. No, we'll reconcile . . .

We had a quick chat about it before the Court Case came up and when they called our names we had to still go in and front the judge. After all was said—The Judge turned to Mr John R,M. Hart and said "I'm disgusted in you Mr Hart at taking such young children away from their mother for so long and you are a very lucky man that Miss Brett is willing to give you another chance." Shit, I would have won. Still it's not worth the risk.

Finally, and at long last I got my babies back, my cute little darlings. They were upstairs at the Child minding centre. Mr. Hate was happy. I was completely wrapped. I had a nice present for each of them and in those first few moments of joy and cuddles and crying we were all very happy. I dreaded to think how these two small minds had wondered in all this time what has happened to mummy. To a small child an hour seems like ages and a day seems like forever and 3 weeks and you're forgotten. They had not forgotten completely though. Elliot came running up to me arms outstretched, but my little Larry—pulled away at first. Mr. Hate held him and he pulled back from me. That hurt—that really hurt. My own little boy pulled back from me like he didn't really know me anymore. Oh my God what has Mr. Hate done to them. How much were they hurting all this time? Deep breaths, Nicky. Get through this and out the other side.

Mr. Hate, who hadn't had a smoke in 3 whole weeks, so I couldn't say he was a pot smoker, rolled up a humungus joint as soon as we got in the car. I very carefully asked, "Do you mind if I get three scotches now that I can finally relax?" No Probs. So we went home and became a family once more. Well it looked like a family on the outside and no one else knew, how I really felt.

Now as I had neglected the rent for a couple of times in the last few weeks they sent me an eviction notice. So I had a week and a half at this place and I wanted to go back to the country. I also wanted to try and get near Mum and Dad who were now at the Sunshine Coast.

I mean WE. We wanted to get back to the country. Ha Ha!

Mr. Hate and I will never be WE, not in my mind. Finally after a lot of searching, I found an excellent place 10 minutes out of Gympie with the most outstanding Queenslander on it and for the same bloody price I was paying at suburban, Eagleby. Snapped it up as quick as I could and started the slow process of moving.

Wayne, a mate of mine from Eagleby was staying on the lounge for a few days and so he and his mate gave us a good helping hand here. They also came up to Gympie to help unload. Then they were gonna get a lift back with Mr. Hate who was driving the Rent-a-truck back to Brisbane.

We left my nice little house at Eagleby with the lot packed into the truck and the now going Urvan. I had the 4 kids, the 2 dogs and all the last bits and pieces. Before hitting the Gateway Bridge the van was boiling its guts out. As usual it was me and the kids. I pulled over and waited for the truck to come by and then asked if Wayne wouldn't mind coming with me, because I could not cop this shit box on my own again. If I had broken down on this particular trip alone I would never have got to Gympie. Wayne did come with me and thank Christ for that. It took us six hrs to do a three hour trip, what with all the stopping to cool down and top up the radiator.

I was driving and Wayne was keeping me amused. "Keep going Nick, it's not boiling yet." He'd say. We stopped at Caboulture and got a beer each at some pub and let the dogs out for a walk too, gave the Errrrvan a half hour rest and then off we went again. We were doing the huge speeds of 60kms to 70kms, everyone was overtaking but I just had to keep plodding along.

In that six-hour trip I had more fun and more laughs with Wayne than in months or years with Mr. Hate. I knew I couldn't play this game with him anymore and I could never forgive him for the pain he put me through. **NEVER.** He hurt me so much more than any punch in the head ever could. Emotional pain is more than I could bear and for all that time. Any man who could put the woman he professes to love through this, could not love them. Already I had a friend of mine, Sam, moving in temporarily because her fellow had jut thrown her out with two little boys and I knew I didn't want to live with Mr. Hate. Least of all alone with him, like a marriage situation.

When Wayne and I and the kids finally got there we helped unpack all the stuff from the truck. Then he and Mr. Hate and the other bloke had to take the truck back to Brissy. They returned around 8pm. Sam and I and all the kids had been sitting in the dark in the kitchen telling stories and having a few house warming drinks. When Wayne and Mr. Hate got back the power finally came on and we all sat round enjoying the new place and having a joke or two. I could see in Mr. Hates face he was wishing Wayne and Sam weren't here and I, on the other hand was so glad they were.

I would never change and I knew I would never be Mrs. Hart. We were just too unsuited, it wasn't to be. I would never be happy with him. In fact I'd probably never be happy with anyone. Fuck em' all, they've all been no good for me. Never got me anywhere and never gave me nothing. Nothing but a black eye that is, or grief of some sort.

So as in the Carpenters song:-

So I've made my mind up I must live my life alone.
I know this isn't easy and I guess I've always known.
I'd say goodbye to love.
I'll say goodbye to love.

Now all I hope for is big truckloads of money from my Story and though **Money Can't Buy Me Love,** It can give me happiness.

<u>NAUGHTY NICKERS.</u>